Using Wikis for Online Collaboration

JOSSEY-BASS GUIDES
TO ONLINE TEACHING AND LEARNING

Using Wikis for Online Collaboration

THE POWER OF THE READ-WRITE WEB

James A. West
Margaret L. West

JOSSEY-BASS
A Wiley Imprint
www.josseybass.com

Published by Jossey-Bass
A Wiley Imprint
989 Market Street, San Francisco, CA 94103-1741—www.josseybass.com

Readers should be aware that Internet Web sites offered as citations and/or sources for further information may have changed or disappeared between the time this was written and when it is read.

Limit of Liability/Disclaimer of Warranty: While the publisher and author have used their best efforts in preparing this book, they make no representations or warranties with respect to the accuracy or completeness of the contents of this book and specifically disclaim any implied warranties of merchantability or fitness for a particular purpose. No warranty may be created or extended by sales representatives or written sales materials. The advice and strategies contained herein may not be suitable for your situation. You should consult with a professional where appropriate. Neither the publisher nor author shall be liable for any loss of profit or any other commercial damages, including but not limited to special, incidental, consequential, or other damages.

Jossey-Bass books and products are available through most bookstores. To contact Jossey-Bass directly call our Customer Care Department within the U.S. at 800-956-7739, outside the U.S. at 317-572-3986, or fax 317-572-4002.

Jossey-Bass also publishes its books in a variety of electronic formats. Some content that appears in print may not be available in electronic books.

Library of Congress Cataloging-in-Publication Data

West, James A.
    Using wikis for online collaboration : the power of the read-write web / James A. West, Margaret L. West.
       p.   cm.
    Includes bibliographical references and index.
       ISBN 978-0-470-34333-3 (pbk.)
       1. Computer-assisted instruction.   2. Internet in education.   3. Electronic encyclopedias.
    4. User-generated content.   5. Wikipedia.   I. West, Margaret L.   II. Title.
    LB1028.5.W398   2009
    371.33'44693—dc22
                                                                                        2008038210

Printed in the United States of America
FIRST EDITION
PB Printing   10 9 8 7 6 5 4 3 2 1

CONTENTS

EXHIBITS

FIVE

FIGURES

PREFACE

There is no doubt that the World Wide Web is changing. Since the turn of the twenty-first century, the once-static Web has evolved into the "read-write Web," offering new opportunities for online interaction, collaboration, and learning (Richardson, 2006). The growth of such next-generation Web tools as blogs, social networks, and wikis is astounding, with new collaborative tools appearing online almost daily. Educators are increasingly interested in discovering ways to harness these technologies effectively, both to improve online learning and to promote critical thinking and collaboration.

Collaborative writing tools, such as wikis, are well suited to supporting meaningful learning in online courses. A wiki can be defined as a "collaborative web space where anyone can add content and anyone can edit content that has already been published" (Richardson, 2006, p. 8). Wikis offer a shared environment where online students can actively participate in the integration and co-creation of knowledge. Wiki technology can be harnessed to foster dynamic online learning communities, in which students come together around a shared goal. Wiki community members use the shared space to write, discuss, comment, edit, reflect, and evaluate, with the ultimate goal to complete a shared outcome. Educators must learn to embrace a new "age of participation" and be prepared to coach students in their ability to collaborate online in the creation of products and the sharing of information and learning (Tapscott & Williams, 2006).

Although wikis hold great promise for online learning, without planning, design, and effective facilitation, a wiki is no more than an empty Web page. This book strives to provide educators with useful and practical guidelines, tools, and processes for integrating collaborative wiki projects into online courses. In order to help faculty members embrace the potential of online collaborative writing, we review the nature of wiki technology, explore the pedagogical foundations of online collaborative writing, and present practical examples for wiki projects that support knowledge construction, critical thinking, and contextual learning.

AUDIENCE

This book is primarily intended for those who teach online courses. The focus is on supporting the needs of higher education practitioners, including faculty, instructional designers, and developers of interactive, collaborative online courses. Although this book focuses on the online teaching community, the information and examples provided in this book also apply to those teaching in a blended learning environment.

This book is also intended for students preparing for roles in higher education, instructional technology, and adult education in which online learning plays a part.

OVERVIEW OF THE CONTENTS

This book is designed to be a guide for integrating collaborative wiki projects into online courses. We have kept theoretical material to a minimum, instead placing emphasis on integrating online collaborative writing into instruction using sound pedagogical practices. Chapter One briefly describes the history and development of collaborative Web tools and the nature of the wiki as compared to other forms of asynchronous communication. This chapter also discusses the technology and infrastructure necessary for implementing a wiki, and provides guidelines for comparing and selecting wiki services and software.

Chapter Two discusses the wiki's potential as a collaborative learning environment and explores the suitability of the technology for millennial and adult online students. This chapter addresses preparing online students for success through skills assessment and orientation activities, and outlines the pedagogical considerations for creating wiki projects that support online learning goals. Practical suggestions and tips for planning and designing the wiki project framework and managing the collaborative writing process complete the chapter.

Chapters Three, Four, and Five provide detailed guidelines for framing and facilitating wiki projects for three distinct levels of learning. Chapter Three focuses on projects that support cognitive processing and knowledge construction, emphasizing projects that promote the organization, summary, and integration of information and concepts. Chapter Four concentrates on more complex collaborative activities, with emphasis on critical thinking and analysis. Chapter Five focuses on contextual learning activities for online learning teams; these activities require both synthesis of knowledge and application of skills to real-world contexts and problems.

ACKNOWLEDGMENTS

We thank the faculty and staff at Western Illinois University for providing the resources and encouragement to explore, experiment with, and discover the many uses of wikis in online instruction. We are particularly grateful to our online students, who have been consistently open to new ideas and who have taught us a great deal about the changing nature of higher education in this new, digital world.

A special thanks to Sharon Sample, access and serials librarian at Quincy University, for her vision and for leading us to many useful resources on wikis in education. We also humbly acknowledge the community of educators we have been privileged to learn from every August at the Annual Conference on Distance Teaching and Learning in Madison, Wisconsin. Over the years, we have been both challenged and inspired by this community, and we appreciate the opportunity, in writing this book, to give back some of what we have gained. We thank Erin Null, our editor at Jossey-Bass, for offering us this unique opportunity and for her encouragement and helpful feedback throughout the process. Finally, we offer special thanks to our families and friends, especially our children, who displayed infinite patience and understanding as we became immersed in the research and writing of this book.

ABOUT THE AUTHORS

James (Jim) West is an associate professor in the Department of Instructional Design and Technology at Western Illinois University (WIU). He teaches courses in multimedia instructional design and development, and in using Internet resources for teaching and training. Previously, he has also taught courses in instructional design, performance technology, and library media at Northern Illinois University and Dominican University (River Forest, Illinois).

Jim West holds an Ed.D. in Instructional Technology and a Master's in Library Science from Northern Illinois University, and has over fifteen years of experience in the fields of instructional technology and information science.

Prior to joining the faculty at WIU, he was senior consultant for Performance Systems Design Corp., where he designed and implemented training, distance learning, knowledge management, and curriculum development solutions for companies such as Sears, Unext, and Monsanto.

Jim West regularly presents his research at national and international conferences, including in the United States, Europe, Latin America, and Canada. He has presented at the International Society for Performance Improvement (ISPI), ISPI Europe, the American Society for Training and Development (ASTD), the Association for Educational Communications and Technology (AECT), the International Distance Learning Conference, and the International Essen Symposium.

Margaret (Peggy) West is an instructional technology systems manager in the Center for Innovation in Teaching and Research at Western Illinois University. She is responsible for the development and training of faculty, especially in the areas of pedagogy and distance learning. She has over twenty years of experience as an instructional designer, consultant, and university educator in northern and western Illinois.

Peggy West received her Ph.D. in instructional technology from Kansas State University. She has taught courses in instructional design and distance education at National Louis University (Chicago), Northern Illinois University (NIU), and Western Illinois University. She developed one of the first fully online courses at NIU in 1995.

Peggy West was a senior consultant for Performance Systems Design Corp., where she designed and implemented distance learning and training programs for companies such as Sears, Diamond Technology, and Motorola.

She has presented at national and international conferences of professional associations, including ASTD, ISPI, ISPI Europe, AECT, the Academy of Human Resource Development, and the Annual Distance Learning Conference in Madison, Wisconsin.

chapter ONE

Getting Ready to Wiki

For many years, interactivity on the Web was limited to clicking, browsing, reading, and searching through Web sites and online databases. Web users were passive consumers of online information. However, the original vision and promise of the Web, according to Tim Berners-Lee, developer of the World Wide Web, was the possibility of its providing collaborative online spaces where "we can all meet and read and write" (Carvin, 2005, p. 1). Today, the Web facilitates a new age of participation that is closer to Berners-Lee's original intent, inviting users to participate, co-create, edit, and collaborate, rather than merely consume (Lamb, 2004). We have moved from a read-only Web (Web 1.0) to the read-write Web (Web 2.0).

Web 2.0 tools, such as blogs, wikis, social networking software, media sharing, and others, have been instrumental in shifting the Web to its new identity as a collaborative work space, or digital commons, where "we can all meet to read and write." The digital commons is having an impact in online classrooms, as educators begin to take advantage of free services and the variety of online collaborative tools available. Online educators now have an expanded tool set to support student-centered instruction and collaborative learning. Online students are no longer restricted to passive browsing, page reading, message posting, and other individual learning activities. In the digital commons, online students have the capacity to become collaborative partners in the knowledge-building process.

OPPORTUNITIES FOR ONLINE LEARNING

The timing couldn't be more perfect. Learners in the twenty-first century have been Web consumers for much of their lives, and are now demanding online instruction that supports participation and interaction. They want learning experiences that are social and that will connect them with their peers. They expect activities and content to be relevant to the real world (Beldarrain, 2006). Today's learners expect more than online lectures or one-way communications. Activities that promote interaction and collaboration with their peers are becoming an integral part of how students learn. As a result, many educators are moving away from instructor-centered methods of teaching to more contextual learning and real-world problem-solving techniques. The new Web provides the tools and technologies that can support educators in creating a rich, collaborative learning atmosphere in their online classrooms (Lightner, Bober, & Willi, 2007).

Although some first-generation Web tools such as e-mail, chat, and threaded discussion have allowed for effective online course communication, it has often been a challenge to collaborate using these tools (Palloff & Pratt, 2005). Web 2.0 applications have greater potential for building online collaborative learning communities. Wikis, in particular, are showing great promise for enhancing online learning. Within a wiki, learners possessing little or no knowledge of HTML can collaboratively use, create, and modify Web content. The learning curve for using wikis is generally low, and learning groups given assignments with a solid purpose and clear structure have a high capacity for quickly engaging in knowledge construction, critical thinking, and contextual learning. Although wikis do not replace first-generation communication tools, they extend the online classroom beyond its current limits and boundaries. Online educators are taking notice, and the number adopting wikis grows exponentially every day (Godwin-Jones, 2003).

Before jumping on the wiki bandwagon, educators need to consider the implications these tools will have for both learning and the curriculum. It is important to consider how the available tools differ and how they can be incorporated into the classroom. Educators also need to be familiar with the wiki concept in order to make informed choices when selecting a particular wiki service or software tool. In this chapter, we address the advantages and disadvantages of wiki technology and pose critical questions to consider before you make the leap to integrating wikis into your online course.

WHAT IS A WIKI?

A wiki is an online collaborative writing tool. As defined earlier, a wiki is a "collaborative web space where anyone can add content and anyone can edit content that has already been published" (Richardson, 2006, p. 8). Wikis are designed to help groups collaborate, share, and build online content, and are especially useful for distance learners who are separated by time and place. Wikis present an approach to group writing and editing that is more efficient than forwarding e-mail attachments with tracked changes, a method that supports only one editor at a time and can create issues with students having multiple and conflicting versions of the same document. Wiki documents are available for editing and commenting to all members at all times. No one has to wait for a current file to be forwarded to them. It is easy to track each person's contributions and to maintain a record of all changes and edits (Waters, 2007). Anyone with access, permission, and a Web browser can contribute to a wiki. Members of a wiki can both add new pages and edit existing pages. Many wikis also offer extended editing capabilities and features that enable file sharing, commenting, and embedded discussion.

Although the concept of wikis has been around for many years, the first true wiki, called WikiWikiWeb, was created by Ward Cunningham in 1995 (Tapscott & Williams, 2006). Cunningham used the word *wiki,* derived from the Hawaiian word for "quick," to mean a collection of Web pages that can be edited by anyone. Cunningham was inspired by early hypertext programs like HyperCard, but it wasn't until the development of the World Wide Web that he was able to create the first wiki.

Perhaps the most well-known wiki is Wikipedia (www.wikipedia.org). Wikipedia is a free online encyclopedia with completely open content: nearly every article can be edited by anyone. Since its introduction in 2001, Wikipedia has grown to be the most popular general reference work on the Web. Although there is controversy over the accuracy of its content, there is no doubt of the collaborative nature of Wikipedia. In recent years, the founders of Wikipedia have partnered with other organizations to create the Wikimedia Foundation (wikimediafoundation.org/wiki/Home), a nonprofit organization designed to create multiple open-content sites created using wikis, and to provide those sites to the public free of charge. One of these projects is Wikiversity (www.wikiversity.org), which allows users to create, edit, and share resources across multiple disciplines for use in online learning.

Wikis Versus Other Asynchronous Communication Tools

Wikis are similar to other types of online communication tools, such as blogs and threaded discussions, in that these are all asynchronous forms of communication. In asynchronous communication, contributions are made not in real time but at different times. The similarities end there, however. Blogs, for example, are generally posted by a single author and may or may not invite user comments, yet wikis are specifically designed for multiple authors and group collaboration. Blog messages are posted with a linear construction, displayed chronologically, and typically present no opportunities for other users to edit previous posts. Threaded discussions also support the posting of messages from multiple contributors and, like wikis, can be designed as a means of sharing ideas, providing feedback, and generating conversation around a particular topic. Threaded discussion postings are static, however, and users can only elaborate on existing messages. Wiki pages, conversely, are dynamic and allow participants to add to, change, and even delete someone else's contribution.

Wikis Versus Blogs

A blog, short for Weblog, allows users to create a personal Web site and is an easy tool to implement in online learning. Blogs are well suited to such online activities as reflection, creative expression, and journaling. Most blogs are personal or journalistic. Like wikis, blogs have the potential to expand beyond the boundaries of the online classroom in ways that allow learners to collaborate with learners, experts, practitioners, and other members of a global audience (Godwin-Jones, 2003). There are clear distinctions, however, between these two tools. Blog postings are made in a chronological sequence, with the most recent entries typically displayed at the top of the page. Wikis are organized more dynamically than blogs, with the grouping of information determined by new entries, hyperlinked concepts, and collaboratively determined structures. Further, a blog is typically managed by a single person, who has primary responsibility for the content and structure of the site. Wiki ownership is distributed and shared among all of its contributing members. Finally, and most importantly, blog postings typically cannot be modified, whereas wiki contributions are open for editing.

Wikis Versus Threaded Discussions

Threaded discussion is a mainstay of online course communications. In a threaded discussion, users access a public discussion topic or thread, post messages, and reply to the messages of others. All users who have access to the thread can read the messages. Wikis, similar to discussion forums, provide students with opportunities to elaborate on topics in an asynchronous manner. Both tools have a transparent structure that is visible to all users (Chase, 2007). As is also the case with blogs, however, once messages are posted to a threaded discussion, they typically cannot be edited, except by the original author or discussion administrator. This creates a critical difference between threaded discussions and wikis. Whereas threaded discussion supports elaboration of individual concepts and ideas, wikis allow for students' concepts and ideas to be integrated with those of the rest of the class through collaborative editing (Farabaugh, 2007). Instead of limiting users to adding to another student's contribution, the wiki opens the door to brainstorming, group problem solving, critical evaluation, synthesis, idea refinement, and group consensus.

Wikis have the potential to be more suitable than blogs or threaded discussions for supporting online collaboration, especially among learning teams with a specific, shared goal ("Educator's Guide," 2006). In online courses, blogs and discussion boards are best used as communication tools, while the wiki serves as the learning team's collaborative work space. The overall purpose of a wiki is to support the team's needs for building a shared understanding of a topic, goal, or objective; to support team processes such as planning, research, and problem solving; and to create team outcomes through a shared document or set of documents. Exhibit 1.1 summarizes the differences between wikis, blogs, and threaded discussions.

Exhibit 1.1
Comparison of Asynchronous Communication Tools

Wikis	Blogs	Threaded Discussions
Collaborative authorship	Single author	Multiple authors
Dynamic	Static	Static
Nonlinear and multipage construction	Linear construction	Threaded construction

To Wiki or Not to Wiki . . . ?

As an online instructor, you can choose from many online tools to support your class activities. Keep in mind, however, that your choices do not have to be exclusive. Using a wiki does not mean you have to abandon blogs, threaded discussions, or other useful tools. You can use a wiki in combination with these tools, matching the strengths and features of each with the requirements of the activity at hand.

Wikis are best suited for collaborative activities, especially those that are dynamic and nonlinear in construction and will result in a shared product or outcome. You could choose a wiki for a noncollaborative activity, such as a private journal, but a blog would be more suitable for this type of personal reporting. A threaded discussion could allow for open discussion and limited collaboration, but a wiki would provide more flexibility for students who must work together to develop a group project. The following are examples of activities that lend themselves well to collaboration in a shared wiki:

- Your learners are building an archive of resources on a particular topic.
- Your learners are exploring different sides of an issue by means of a debate.
- Your learners need to work together to create a unified project, such as a collaborative research paper or media design project.

Although it is possible to build an entire online course within a wiki, it is not recommended. It can be much more powerful to combine the collaborative nature of the wiki with other online course tools. For example, if you adopt a wiki to support a collaborative activity, such as an online debate, learners could construct and edit the two sides of the debate in the wiki, share opinions and summarize issues that were addressed in the debate in a threaded discussion topic, and vote on which side "won" the debate in an interactive survey or poll. You could also provide additional links to course materials or outside resources.

TYPES OF WIKIS

Once you have decided to use a wiki, where do you find the one that will work best with your online course? Wikis are available through a wide variety of services and open-source software tools, and generally fall into three categories, each with its own set of strengths and limitations:

- Free wiki services
- Fee-based wiki services
- Self-hosted wikis

Free Wiki Services

Free wiki services are available at no cost through a wiki provider, such as Google Docs (http://docs.google.com) or WetPaint (www.wetpaint.com). Wiki pages are hosted and accessed from the wiki service's Web servers and require no local software installation. They are usually very easy to set up and administer. Most free services limit the number of members that can edit the wiki or the number of pages that can be created, but most offer a reasonable amount of storage space for getting started with small wiki projects. Many free services have the option of alerting the administrator whenever a page on the wiki has been edited. Free services tend to have limited administrative capabilities, however, particularly when it comes to passwords, security, and controlling access to individual wiki pages or folders.

Fee-Based Wiki Services

Fee-based wikis are also hosted and accessed from the wiki service's Web servers. These services offer expanded features based on the type of subscription you select. Features may include more advanced management capabilities, more storage, or added security. In addition, fee-based services typically allow a larger, or even unlimited, number of members and pages. Most subscription services allow the administrator to add and link groups, and to control user access to specific pages in the wiki. Like the free wiki services, fee-based wikis are often very easy to use, requiring minimal technical experience and no software installation. On the downside, subscription services incur a monthly or annual cost, and you must keep subscriptions up to date in order to maintain administrative controls.

Self-Hosted Wikis

Wiki software can also be installed directly on a personal or campus-controlled server space. A variety of free, open-source wiki software is available for download from the Internet, for example, MediaWiki (www.mediawiki.org/wiki/MediaWiki) and TWiki (www.twiki.org/). Self-hosting a wiki allows for maximum control over access and security, and typically provides much more storage space than is available through free or fee-based services. This approach, however, can have clear disadvantages for online educators. You must first have the server space allotted to the wiki. You must also have the necessary technical expertise to customize and administer the software. Self-hosted wikis may also require additional end-user training, depending on the unique requirements of the wiki software. Exhibit 1.2 summarizes the strengths and limitations of the different types of wiki services.

Exhibit 1.2
Strengths and Limitations of Wiki Services

Free Services	Fee-Based Services	Self-Hosting
Strengths	**Strengths**	**Strengths**
No cost	Advanced management capabilities	Usually allow maximum amount of control
Quick start-up	Added security	More secure
Easy to monitor	Large or unlimited number of members and pages	
Minimal technical experience required	Easy to add and link groups	
	Minimal technical experience required	
	More secure	
Limitations	**Limitations**	**Limitations**
Minimal management capabilities	Some cost involved, usually through a subscription	Must have own server
Least amount of security	May require more planning and time to set up	Some technical and networking experience necessary
Some limitations on number of members or pages		Often require more end-user training
		More start-up time

Wikis in Learning Management Systems

Some learning management systems (LMS) have built-in wiki tools. The strengths and limitations of these can be compared to both free services (because they generally incur no cost) and self-hosted wikis (because they are locally supported). Like free wikis, LMS wiki tools are relatively easy to add to the online course and typically offer basic editing and formatting features. Most offer single-page constructions and are automatically "private" to the students who have access to the LMS. Similar to self-hosted wikis, LMS wiki tools are hosted on a local campus LMS server and are maintained by campus technology support personnel. Blackboard, Moodle, and several other LMS systems include wikis as part of their overall course systems.

CHOOSING THE RIGHT WIKI

With all of the options available, how do you decide which is the right wiki for your online course? There is no doubt that a premium, fee-based wiki service offers all the bells and whistles you can imagine. Self-hosted wikis are also unlimited in what they can do. But do you really need a Cadillac if a Volkswagen will do the job? The first question you should ask is, "What do I want my students to do with the wiki?" How you answer this question will help you determine the features that you need to accomplish your goals. The following questions will help you set priorities and narrow the field of choices to a more focused set of alternatives:

Key Features

- How many people will be using the wiki?
- Do I need to have separate groups?
- Will these groups need to have access to one another's pages?
- How secure do the pages need to be?
- Should the pages be public or private?
- What amount of administrative control will I need?

Ease of Use

- How skilled are my learners at using a computer and navigating the Web?
- Do my learners need to know how to use HTML?
- How concerned am I about formatting and page layout?

Cost

- Do I have the money to pay for a fee-based wiki service?

- Is it necessary to subscribe to a service, or can I accomplish my goals with a free service?

- Will advertisements cause a distraction to my learners?

Support

- Do I have the technical skills to install and set up a self-hosted wiki?

- Is technical support available if I do not have the skills?

- Will I have the necessary server space if I choose to self-host?

- How quickly do I need to set up my wiki?

Once your priorities are clear, compare specific wiki software and services. Visit the home pages of several services and view available demos and tutorials. Play in the wiki "sandbox" if one is available. A sandbox is an active wiki page that allows users to practice with the various features of a wiki, without the fear of making any mistakes. Since a sandbox is just like any other wiki page, you will have the opportunity to sample all of the features the wiki has to offer.

FEATURES OF WIKIS

Before selecting a particular wiki, it is important to be familiar with the features that distinguish one wiki service from another. Wikis can differ in how they handle security and login access, backups and archives, and server space (Lamb, 2004). Wiki Matrix (www.wikimatrix.org) is an excellent resource for comparing the features of different wikis (see Figure 1.1).

When determining which wiki to use and how to incorporate it into the online classroom, consider the following:

Access Controls

Wikis can be either "public" or "private." A public wiki is one that is visible to anyone on the Web, without their having to log in. Search engines will often identify these pages and include them in their databases. Users then can discover the wiki by searching on the Web. It's easy to spread the word by sharing the wiki's URL through e-mail, or by providing a direct link to the wiki on a Web site.

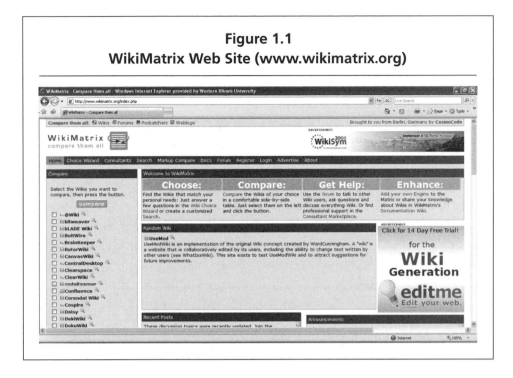

Figure 1.1
WikiMatrix Web Site (www.wikimatrix.org)

A private wiki is visible only to those who have password access to it, or who have been "invited" to join the wiki by someone who has password access. Many wiki services allow you to invite other users to your wiki. This is often done by entering the users' e-mail addresses. Then the wiki sends an e-mail, which contains a special link to those users. Search engines will not see the pages, and they won't appear when users search on terms that might otherwise provide a link to the page. In addition, if someone comes across your wiki's URL, either through a link on a different Web site or by some other means, they will not be able to view the wiki. They will instead see a login page or a password request before they can gain access to the wiki.

Most free and fee-based wiki services allow you to choose whether or not you want your wiki to be public or private. Some allow you to change these permissions after wiki creation. Self-hosted wikis can exist behind a firewall or on an internal secure server. These wikis are not accessible to anyone outside of the firewall. They may use server authentication so that only restricted users can access, edit, or manage the pages.

Capacity

All wikis support the creation of multiple pages by multiple authors, and thus can quickly grow in size. Depending on the wiki, there may be restrictions on how many pages you can create, the length of each page, and the size of embedded images and media. For fee-based or free wikis, there may be a limit to the total storage space your wiki is allowed to occupy on the host's server. The higher the level of your service, the greater the number of pages and overall available storage space you can use. Services are competitive, and Web storage is becoming less and less expensive, so check and compare subscription services often to get the most capacity for your money.

Free wiki services generally allow the fewest number of pages and the smallest amount of storage space. Capacity is not a problem for wiki projects that involve only a few learners, creating a limited number of pages. Some free wikis offer bonuses, such as increasing the number of pages allowed, when additional users are invited to participate in the wiki or if the wiki is made public. Capacity is becoming less of a problem as the cost of storage space goes down. Unless the wiki includes a large number of media files or attachments, the wiki projects in Chapters Three through Five of this book can all be accomplished with a free wiki service.

In wikis that are self-hosted, the storage capacity of your local server determines the limits. The ability to install hard drives with hundreds of gigabytes of storage effectively means that self-hosted wikis can have an unlimited number of pages. Self-hosted wikis have the advantage of being readily able to expand or contract according to the changing needs of your online courses.

Editing Features

Although wikis offer a variety of features that allow users to change the wiki's page layout, organization, and formatting, a wiki is not Microsoft Word! Basic word processing features, such as fonts, bullets, and simple tables, are available in most wikis and are generally easy to use. Adding complex tables or other layouts is often difficult to accomplish in a wiki. Some wikis add extra editing and formatting features when you upgrade from a free service to a fee-based service. For example, pbWiki (www.pbWiki.com) provides the ability to use customized cascading style sheets (CSS) in the platinum-level wiki package. Google Docs includes a very powerful page editor compared to many other wikis. Google Docs also allows learners to create pages offline using Microsoft Office products, including Word, Excel, and PowerPoint, and then to upload the documents directly into the wiki. Most wikis allow users to edit pages in HTML mode through a "view source" option; however, the real strength of the wiki lies in the fact that users don't have to know HTML code to be able to edit and format a wiki page.

Customization and Skins

One challenge with wikis is that pages have a tendency to look plain and generic. Customizing the way a wiki looks is often limited by the editing features of the wiki or by the various "skins" that you can use. A skin is an overlaying page design theme that affects the default fonts and colors on the wiki pages. Self-hosted wikis allow you to create your own skins, but this will require some technical and Web-design expertise. Free and fee-based wikis often provide a limited number of skins with their wikis. In pbWiki, for example, the number of skins increases when you upgrade from a free wiki to one of their premium services. The advantage of multiple skins is that your learners have the ability to take control over how their wiki looks. Having multiple skins does not change how learners add and edit content on the wiki, however, and has little effect on how you administer the wiki and incorporate it into your course.

Advertising

Free wiki services typically include advertising on their pages, which you cannot remove. For example, WetPaint includes ads that appear below the menu on the left and at the bottom of the page. Generally, these ads are not overwhelming, but they may become a distraction to your learners. Upgrades to fee-based wikis will often include the removal of ads as an incentive. Of course, self-hosted wikis are completely free from advertising.

Communication

Most wikis support some type of embedded communication among wiki members. This can take the form of e-mail links to members, discussion threads, and page comments. The ability to communicate with other members within the wiki can be instrumental to the success of an online wiki project. WetPaint, for example, offers threaded discussions for every page in the wiki. This gives learners the ability to relate conversations and discussions to a particular wiki page or topic. WetPaint also allows users to create new threads on any added wiki page.

Self-hosted wikis, such as MediaWiki, provide a discussion tab that is always available to wiki members and visitors. Other wiki services enable users to comment on pages, but do not offer threaded discussions. Depending on the types of wiki activities you want to integrate into your online course, you may need to look closely at embedded communications before choosing your wiki service. If embedded communication is not available, consider how you might use your course management system in tandem with the wiki to provide learning teams with additional communication channels.

File Sharing

Although all wikis support hyperlinks to documents and Web sites already located on the Web, some wikis support file sharing within the wiki through a file upload feature. Such files as images, media, PDF documents, and spreadsheets can be linked to, or embedded within, a wiki page. Some wikis provide a "sidebar" area for related files and hyperlinks. As you might guess, the amount of storage space you have for uploading files will depend on the level of your wiki service, with free wikis having the least amount of space. File-sharing capabilities within a wiki are important, if part of your wiki learning activity involves sharing many files with other users. One example of this is a wiki project that includes creating a resource bank of PowerPoint files that students need to share with one another.

Administration

Administration of a wiki involves planning for how learners will access and use the wiki, and ensuring the security of the learners and their wiki contributions. It is important, for example, to determine your requirements for the number of users, logins, and passwords; archiving and version control; and security.

Wikis provide various levels of administrative capabilities that control user access, group setup, passwords, and version control. Free services have minimal administrative capabilities. For example, in pbWiki, the wiki creator is the only person who can delete pages or files. The wiki creator also controls the password for logging into the wiki. Free services typically have one main login and password. The administrator can invite others to participate in the wiki, but no additional passwords are assigned. Most wiki services also offer higher-end, fee-based options, which allow the creation of multiple user accounts and access controls for specific pages.

Number of Users Some wiki services limit the number of users that can be members of a wiki. This has usually been the case with free wikis. The trend has been to remove these user limits, however, even for the free wiki sites. For example, pbWiki no longer limits the numbers of users. Fee-based and self-hosted wikis typically do not limit the number of users.

Logins and Passwords All wikis provide some measure of control over access through the use of login and password protection. As you can imagine, free wiki services provide the most basic access control, and self-hosted services offer the greatest ability to customize access. Fee-based services offer various levels of password protection, depending on the wiki service and the level of service that you purchase.

The most basic level of password protection involves a general password to read and write on pages in the wiki. Most free services offer this level of password protection. The administrator of the wiki often has the ability to keep the password secret: other users of the wiki access the site through an invitation, which acts as a customized link to the wiki and serves the same purpose as providing a password. The benefit of this option is that you can quickly share a wiki with different users, without having to share the password. The drawback is that there is only one password, with one level of access. Anyone with the password has the ability to read and edit any page on the site.

A second option is to use a wiki service that has more administrative control over password and page access. This is not typically available in free wikis. The benefit, however, is that the instructor can create password groups that allow groups to read and edit some, but not all, of the pages. This method can be very effective when you are working with several different groups on related projects. You may want the entire class to see what their peers are doing but only be able to edit the pages controlled by the group to which they belong.

Self-hosted wikis provide whatever access control you may require. This level of control is often dependent on internal server information, however, and it may take considerable time for technology support personnel to create and manage login and access controls.

Archiving and Version Control The most common concern new wiki contributors express is the fear that they will "mess up" someone else's work. It is not unusual for students to insert edits into the wrong place on a wiki page or accidentally delete material that they wanted to keep. Fortunately, most wikis are set up to easily view the wiki history and to restore prior versions, just in case users overwrite or change text that they want to keep. Wikis typically save versions after each edit, and allow users to compare different versions. Members also have the ability to copy and paste from a prior version into the current version, and the administrator can simply restore an earlier version if necessary. This built-in version control protects against inadvertent errors or deletion of content (Engstrom & Jewett, 2005). Further, because the pure nature of the wiki as an editable environment makes it very easy to remove spam content and graffiti, few hackers waste their time on these activities. Watchful group members with a strong sense of ownership will easily be able to maintain the integrity of the wiki (Lamb, 2004).

Security   It is important that teachers be aware of the risks and challenges that the read-write Web presents. They must consider issues of privacy and safety to ensure that students have the best possible learning experience ("Educator's Guide," 2006). Faculty may worry that someone outside the course will insert random spam or graffiti messages into their wiki projects. This outsider intrusion rarely occurs, however, and can be prevented using the wiki's administrative features (Bold, 2006). Wikis usually have built-in safety measures to guard against malicious use, many of which we have already discussed, including password protection, version archiving, and version control (Godwin-Jones, 2003). An instructor can regulate a wiki so that learners may only edit their own work. However, that tends to defeat the purpose of the wiki as a tool for open collaboration and instructors should avoid doing this. Both the instructor and students must be willing to accept the risks involved in working in a collaborative environment, relinquish ownership, and cede control to the group (Lamb, 2004).

Widgets and RSS Feeds

Wikis are continually updating their services to include additional features through the use of widgets. Widgets are small programs embedded within Web pages that can add functionality and interactivity to wiki pages. Widgets, including media players, games, and interactive calendars, are designed to be easily incorporated into your page. Widgets are often made using Adobe Flash or JAVA. A widget may be created by a wiki service, but more often it is built by third-party services who then make them available to the wiki. WetPaint has an extensive set of widgets that you can easily add to your wiki pages. WetPaint's current widgets include Google Calendars, Google Video (video.google.com) and YouTube video (www.youtube.com), Vizu Polls (www.vizu.com), and the Imeem Music Player (www.imeem.com). Widgets are not limited to those that the wiki service provides; most services allow you to upload widgets from other sources.

One important type of widget that many wiki services offer is an RSS feed that you can incorporate into your wiki page. RSS, which stands for Really Simple Syndication, allows users to subscribe to a page or Web site and be informed automatically when a page has been added or updated. RSS feeds can be used to monitor a news site or keep track of someone's blog entries.

Widgets are useful in that they have the potential to add flexibility and interactivity to a wiki page. For example, you could have a wiki in which group learners are monitoring developments in an election. A key resource could be a news Web site like MSNBC (www.msnbc.msn.com/), and you might set up a widget on your wiki page that consists of an RSS feed of a particular topic at MSNBC. As new articles on your topic are posted at MSNBC, the widget on your wiki is automatically updated.

SETTING UP THE WIKI

When you are finally ready to take the plunge, setting up a wiki is relatively simple and involves three basic steps:

1. Select a wiki service.

2. Determine the wiki's URL.

3. Invite contributors.

Select a Wiki Service

Given the variety of available services, there is a wiki that is right for you. It is important to remember that you do not need to be an expert with servers or wiki software to get a wiki up and running. Many colleges and universities are already running a wiki tool on campus, either through a self-hosted program, such as MediaWiki, or through their learning management system (LMS), such as Blackboard or Moodle. It is worth the time to check with your university's computing support department to see if they have a wiki solution already available to you. If your campus does not have a wiki solution already installed, such free wiki services as Google Docs (http://docs.google.com), WetPaint (www .wetpaint.com), Wikispaces (www.wikispaces.com), or pbWiki (www.pbWiki.com) provide simple wiki solutions that can serve the needs of many small group wiki projects. Once you have selected your wiki service, visit its home page and follow the on-screen directions to create a new wiki.

Determine the Wiki's URL

If you are using your campus LMS wiki service, or if your campus has installed wiki software like MediaWiki, the URL will be automatically provided to you. If you are using a free or fee-based wiki service, you will have to name the URL for your wiki. You may need to set up an account first, which involves providing your e-mail address and setting up your personal password. Most wiki services

Figure 1.2
pbWiki Wiki Creation Page (www.pbWiki.com)

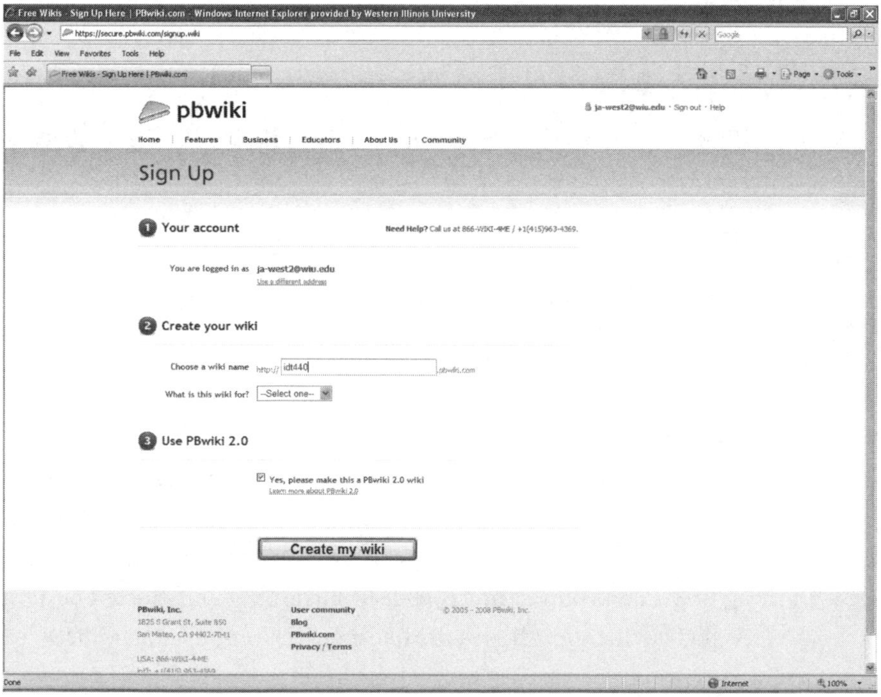

automate this process as part of creating the wiki. For example, pbWiki prompts you to choose a wiki name. You should select something that is unique to your class, such as "IDT440." PbWiki will then check to make sure that URL is not being used by someone else. If the URL is available, you will be given a URL like this: "http://IDT440.pbWiki.com." Figure 1.2 shows the wiki setup page in pbWiki.

Invite Contributors

Once you have created your wiki, you need to invite your students to the wiki. Depending on your wiki service, you can either set up passwords for individual groups or use the wiki service's invite feature. You invite students to your wiki by providing the wiki service with the students' e-mail addresses. The wiki will then send an e-mail to those you invite, containing a special link that automatically logs them into your wiki. The advantage of using the invite feature is that you don't need to worry about setting up passwords for individuals or groups; the wiki manages access for you through the e-mail link.

SUMMARY

With the emergence of the read-write Web, online students have the capacity to become collaborative partners in the knowledge-building process. Wikis and other collaborative software tools have opened the door to new ways of fostering interaction and collaboration in the online classroom. Wikis are unique in that they allow members to create content as well as edit other members' ideas and contributions. Wikis come in a wide variety of shapes and sizes: some are free, some are provided through subscription services, and some can be installed on your local server. You don't need to be an expert to begin using wikis in your online classroom. By selecting an appropriate, free wiki service, or by using your university's or learning management system's existing wiki solution, getting started with a wiki can usually be accomplished with minimal time, training, or support. Now that you have set up your wiki, you are ready to begin designing and framing the wiki project. Although getting started with a wiki can be easy, designing and facilitating a wiki project for online learning is often a bigger challenge. In Chapter Two, we provide an effective process for designing wiki projects for collaborative learning and discuss best practices for managing the wiki. We address the pedagogy of online collaborative writing and offer specific guidelines for planning, designing, facilitating, and managing a successful wiki project in your online course.

Designing Wiki Projects for Collaborative Learning

Although online courses provide opportunities to students who might not otherwise have access to higher education, online students face a variety of challenges unknown to their face-to-face counterparts (Buono, 2004). The challenges increase exponentially when collaborative group work is added to the mix. Without context and support, online groups can experience unbalanced participation, a lack of progress and direction, mistrust, misunderstandings, and conflicts.

Given these factors, simply making an empty wiki available to online students is not enough (Mindel & Verma, 2006). A successful wiki project must take into account the learning outcomes and goals of the project and the unique process of wiki collaboration. Educators must know how to frame wiki activities such that they lead to meaningful learning. During the process of collaboration, educators must learn to take facilitative roles, in which they prepare students for wiki collaboration, facilitate group progress, and manage conflicts and distractions.

TEACHING AND LEARNING THROUGH WIKIS

The ultimate goal of online education is to provide experiences to students that lead to meaningful learning. Educators today understand that meaningful learning cannot be accomplished solely through passive activities such as reading and listening. According to constructivist theory, meaning is gained through active learning, social interaction, and the construction of knowledge (see, for example,

Bruner, 1990; Fink, 2003; Jonassen, Howland, Marra, & Crismond, 2007). Constructivist theory also suggests that meaningful learning is dependent on a rich and relevant context. Contextual Teaching and Learning, an instructional systems theory that schools and higher educational reform movements are steadily adopting, is "based on the premise that meaning emerges from the relationship between content and its context. Context gives meaning to content" (Johnson, 2002, p. 3).

As such, according to contextual teaching and learning principles, the role of the instructor is *not* to provide *learning*. The role of the instructor is to provide the *context* in which learning can occur. Contextual teaching and learning engages students in significant and relevant activities that help them connect their academic learning to real-life situations and problems.

A wiki project can provide the tools and the collaborative work space that enable contextual teaching and learning. The instructor adds context to the basic wiki environment through:

- Establishing a purpose for the wiki project
- Defining and classifying the wiki project's learning goals
- Designing a rich context and problem (through a process called "framing") that support the achievement of the purpose and goals
- Preparing students for work in the new environment
- Promoting a collaborative process through which active, social learning can take place

Johnson (2002) suggests that when students are provided with a rich context and the tools for learning, they achieve higher levels of learning, see a stronger relevance between the problems in the classroom and the problems of the real world, and are more satisfied with the learning experience. When students formulate projects or identify interesting problems, when they make choices and accept responsibility, when they search out information and reach conclusions, when they actively choose, order, organize, touch, plan, investigate, question, and make decisions to reach objectives, they connect academic content to the context of life's situations, and in this way discover meaning.

LAYING THE FOUNDATION—PREPARING STUDENTS FOR WIKI WORK

As discussed in Chapter One, the read-write Web has emerged as a "digital commons": a highly accessible, shared, participatory environment, in which contextual teaching and learning can take place. In the digital commons, students can engage with real people and real problems in a dynamic and evolving work space. Collaborative Web tools, such as wikis, are "changing how companies and societies harness knowledge and capability to innovate and create value" (Tapscott & Williams, 2006, p. 20).

Learning in the Digital Commons

According to Tapscott and Williams (2006), working and learning in the digital commons requires four key behaviors.

Being Open   Openness is an invitation to scrutiny by others. It is the attitude that invites collaboration and seeks out feedback and improvement from others. Being open requires a relinquishing of the self and an appreciation for networking, diversity, new ideas, and alternative approaches to learning and solving problems. In the world of wikis, being open means not only allowing others to comment on your contributions but also welcoming edits, modifications, and additions to your ideas.

Peering   Peering can be defined as a form of organization that seeks "unlikely partners" rather than relying on top-down hierarchies or formal authorities. Peering is based on seeking out and assembling the right talents, information, and resources needed to get a job done. In learning environments, peering is evident when teams self-organize around the learning goal or outcome, and tap into collaborators within and outside of the online classroom.

Sharing   In the digital commons, ownership and intellectual property take on new meanings. In the digital commons, no one person is individually responsible for any of the outcomes. Ideas are shared. Goals are shared. In the case of wikis, the online work space is shared. The outcomes, and even the rewards, are shared. This is, perhaps, the most radical idea that students and online educators must embrace in preparing to learn in this new, collaborative context.

Acting Globally   Although this last principle has, perhaps, more impact on business than on learning environments, global access and awareness are nevertheless hallmarks of the digital commons. Working and learning in the digital commons support the ability to create outcomes that benefit communities and the world at large, extending online classroom boundaries literally "world wide."

Given these requirements, are your students ready to wiki? Do they have the basic skills and characteristics necessary for successful online collaborative writing? Before you begin to integrate a wiki project into your online course, you may first want to consider the characteristics of your students and develop a plan for preparing and orienting them to this new learning environment.

Millennial Students and Online Collaboration

Students born after 1982, often called millennials or the Net Generation, have unique approaches to how they learn and to how they fit information and technology into their lives. In many ways, because of their extended exposure to the Web and other information technologies, millennials are already "wired" for online collaborative writing. There are some characteristics of this audience, however, that can pose challenges to successful wiki work. According to Diana and James Oblinger (2005), the following characteristics have an impact on how millennials approach learning.

Digitally Literate Millennials have grown up with the Web, and intuitively use a variety of information technologies in their daily lives. Millennials are more able than previous generations to express themselves visually and through a variety of media. Although their visual and media literacies are strong, their text literacy and writing skills may actually be less developed.

Connected Millennials have always lived in a world that is highly mobile, and in which information is accessible from any location. They expect constant and reliable access to friends, information, learning, and support.

Immediate This generation likes speed. They often multitask, leaving one task for another whenever things slow down. They prefer instant feedback, instant messaging, and instant delivery. This characteristic can work both in tandem— and in conflict—with other preferences for rich learning experiences, engagement, and meaningful social interaction.

Experiential Most millennial learners prefer to learn by doing, and are impatient with passive activity. They typically enjoy exploring new tools, especially alongside peers. They are rarely intimidated by a new technology or tool.

Social Millennials are constant communicators and tend to be more open to diversity, differences, and sharing than previous generations. They are at ease when meeting new people, both in person and online, and in extending their circle of friends. They are strikingly open about themselves, their opinions, and their emotions. In online collaboration, this can be a double-edged sword, making early communications easier while also opening the door to a wide variety of distractions and off-task discussions.

Teams Millennials prefer to work in teams and often seek out peers for validation and feedback. Even when assigned individual work, millennials will turn to peers for help.

Structure Although some of these characteristics may suggest that they are flexible learners, millennials are, in reality, very achievement oriented, craving boundaries, rules, and procedures. They have a strong preference for structure and pragmatism over ambiguity.

Engagement and Experience If rules and procedures aren't apparent, millennials are not afraid to ask questions, engage others, and seek out answers. They prefer active involvement and tend to be much more willing to "do" than to "stop and reflect."

Things That Matter Millennials tend to be more globally aware than the previous generation and prefer to work on projects with real meaning and relevance. They believe they can make a difference in their communities and are not intimidated by difficult problems.

Working Adults and Nontraditional Students

Working adults and nontraditional students, who are often attracted to online courses because of the convenience and the opportunity to integrate coursework into their already busy lives, display a set of characteristics that contrast those of their younger, millennial-student counterparts. Adult learners are generally more goal oriented than younger students, and are typically more resistant to activities they deem impractical or irrelevant (Knowles, 1984). According to Malcolm Knowles, adult learners tend to possess the following characteristics.

Autonomous and Self-Directed Unlike younger students, who prefer more structured learning environments, adult learners tend to be independent and often prefer to have more control over their own learning. Younger students are generally more social and engage peers to gain deeper understanding, whereas adults tend to engage in self-directed research to clarify a task or topic.

Experienced   Adults bring more work and education experience to the learning process than do younger students, and are consistently seeking opportunities to connect current learning to their existing worldviews. They want to be respected for what they already know and for the experiences they have already undergone. Adult learners tend to have strong, closely held beliefs, which can make them seem resistant to new ideas. In order to consider new ideas and approaches, adults must see the relevance and practicality of change before they will adopt it.

Practical and Goal Oriented   Adults usually are not interested in knowledge for its own sake. Adults typically enroll in continuing or higher education courses to fulfill personal and professional goals. They prefer learning experiences that are achievement oriented and that can be broken down into specific tasks and useful outcomes.

Relevancy Oriented   Adults must see a reason and purpose for their learning in order to fully engage with the instruction. Learning has to be applicable to their work or other responsibilities to be of value to them. They prefer to have choices, alternatives, and opportunities to direct their learning toward topics of personal and professional interest.

Given these characteristics, millennial students and working adults will bring different strengths to a wiki project. Both prefer learning that is active and participatory, rather than passive. Both prefer learning problems that are practical and relevant to the real world over abstract learning exercises. Millennials will be more likely to "dive in" to the wiki on day one, whereas adults will be more likely to self-organize and break the wiki project into specific goals and outcomes. Millennials will be more likely to value social collaboration during the process. Adults will be more capable writers and editors.

Skills and Abilities Required for Wiki Work

Although the existing literature on learning in the digital commons and on the nature of online collaborative writing is relatively slim, case studies and qualitative reports have suggested several characteristics as keys to wiki success (see, for example, Mader, 2008; Tapscott & Williams, 2006; Richardson, 2006; Sharples,

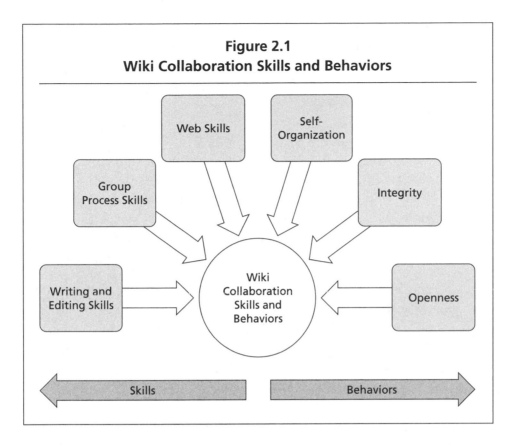

Figure 2.1
Wiki Collaboration Skills and Behaviors

1993). Successful online collaborative writing is dependent not only on cognitive skills, such as Web skills and writing, but also on a number of affective, or values-based, behaviors. Figure 2.1 illustrates the skills and behaviors that have emerged from this growing body of literature.

Cognitive Skills Also called prerequisite skills, these are the basic fundamental skills that students will need in any wiki project.

Writing and Constructive Editing Skills Every wiki project is, at its heart, a collaborative writing project dependent upon skills in research, writing, and editing. A wiki project will require that students be able to use clear and concise written language to communicate. This emphasis on writing can make a wiki project more of a challenge for ESL students, students with writing deficiencies, and students with reading or learning disabilities. To ease the process, help all wiki team members understand that writing is a process that progresses through phases of brainstorming, outlining, elaboration, editing, and refinement. Further, to facilitate the process, help students understand constructive editing: both how to edit and when to edit. This topic is discussed in more depth later in this chapter.

Web Skills   Every wiki project is fully constructed on the Web. Students will, therefore, need to be reasonably comfortable with accessing the Internet, using Web browsers, tracking logins and passwords, writing with embedded wiki HTML editors, and working with digital images or other Web media. Experienced online students will be well versed in at least some of these Web skills. Nevertheless, it is useful, at the start of a project, to gain a clear understanding of each student's confidence and skill with Web-based technologies.

Group Process Skills   These skills tend to vary the most from student to student and group to group. According to Johnson and Johnson (2006), to be effective, group members must be able to set goals; communicate clearly; share leadership, participation, power, and influence; make effective decisions; engage in constructive controversy; and negotiate conflict. It is likely that students have a variety of both negative and positive group learning experiences in their past. It is also likely that students will be stronger in one group process skill than in others. Stimulating a discussion around the question, "What makes a good team?" at the beginning of any wiki learning project can reveal students' strengths and prior group experiences.

Personal Characteristics   In addition to cognitive skills, each group member will bring a set of values and personal characteristics to the project. As discussed earlier, millennial students and working adults have developed these characteristics through prior development, learning, and work experiences. The following are characteristics that stand out in the literature as keys to successful online collaboration:

Openness   Openness is probably the most challenging characteristic required in a wiki project. As suggested by Tapscott and Williams (2006), working in a wiki opens up each contributor's ideas to scrutiny and criticism. Students in a wiki project must be open, not only to suggestions but also to others' modifying, reorganizing, and improving their contributions. Group members must be willing to relinquish and share control over the work space, trusting that the combined talents of the team will create a stronger final product than one member could accomplish alone.

Integrity The group's ability to build trust is largely dependent upon the integrity (or trustworthiness) of each of its members (Duarte & Snyder, 2001). Integrity can be perceived in several ways: through the accountability of each student (for example, the student does what he says he is going to do), through the honesty of each student (for example, the student says what he means), and through the competence of each student's contributions (for example, the student's contributions are accurate and demonstrate knowledge or expertise). Because a wiki project is completed online and often without the benefit of real-time dialogue, this integrity must come through in the student's written communication and wiki contributions.

Self-Organization Self-organization is the ability to see and adjust your own behavior in relation to your environment. Students who engage in self-organization, according to Johnson, "assume responsibility for their own decisions and conduct, appraise alternatives, make choices, develop plans, analyze information, create solutions, and critically evaluate evidence" (2002, p. 34). Self-organization requires metacognition, self-assessment, and the ability to adjust to environmental feedback. In a wiki, this ability lays the foundation for effective collaboration. Groups with the ability to self-organize are more flexible, adaptable, and able to respond to each other. They more easily adjust to the wiki environment and respond swiftly to the project's changing demands.

Instructor Readiness

Given the above requirements, instructors may feel that their students are more ready for wiki work than they are. Online instructors can take some simple steps to prepare themselves for their roles in designing and facilitating a wiki project (Gordon & Stephens, 2007). Begin by focusing on the cognitive skills and personal characteristics described above, particularly in the areas of Web skills and group process skills. Creating and managing a wiki takes little more Web skill than most online educators are already using in discussion forums and learning management tools. "Making a simple wiki is really a snap, especially if you devote just a bit of time to getting your hands dirty in the sandbox" (Gordon & Stephens, 2007, p. 42).

In preparing this book, we surveyed a small group of our faculty colleagues, who have been working with wikis in their online courses. We asked them, "What advice would you have for online faculty who are just beginning to prepare to integrate wikis into their online courses?" Here is a summary of their responses:

- Get familiar and comfortable with the read-write Web. In addition to examining wikis, take a look at what other educators are doing with blogs, social networking, and other interactive Web technologies.

- Look at a wide variety of wiki samples for ideas and to envision possibilities.

- Have a clear idea of what your chosen wiki environment can and cannot do. Don't expect formatting and layout from your students' projects that the wiki won't be able to deliver.

- Create and play in a wiki "sandbox." Experiment with inserting text, images, hyperlinks, and tables. Engage in discovery and experimentation.

- View your wiki in different browsers and on different computers. Become familiar with how different students might experience the wiki environment.

- Be prepared for student questions. Locate and link to the wiki's help pages or Frequently Asked Questions, or construct your own to address questions such as:

  - How do I log into the wiki?

  - What happens if I modify the page without logging in?

  - Can I invite other people to collaborate on the wiki?

  - How do I restore an earlier version if I make a significant mistake?

- Be prepared to support self-organization and to relinquish control. As one faculty member put it, "Be ready to establish the framework for the project, and then get out of the way."

Preparing Students

Student preparation for wiki work should begin well before the first day of the online course. Preparation includes managing student expectations, stimulating relevant skills and attitudes, and orienting students to the new learning environment. Wiki preparation strategies can be integrated into the pre-course activities many online instructors are already using. The following are specific suggestions to help prepare students for wiki collaboration:

- Integrate wiki concepts and expectations into pre-course communications and the online course syllabus. It is important that students consider the educational value and purpose of the wiki project and clearly see its relevance to overall course goals.

- If you require students to complete a pre-course survey, integrate questions related to Web skills, collaboration, and group work. This information can be useful in identifying students who may require additional coaching, as well as in guiding the placement of students into groups.

- Help students answer the question, "What is a wiki?" well before the project begins. In the course syllabus, include links to online resources that help introduce the wiki concept. We have found the "Wiki" article in Wikipedia (http://en.wikipedia.org/wiki/Wiki) to be one of the best resources for this, as it is kept current and provides many related links.

- Create a sandbox or practice page in the wiki, in which students can discover, play in, and test out your chosen environment. This could be as simple as making available to students the sample wiki you created for your own preparation. Later in this chapter, we'll also look at trial runs and icebreakers that can establish trust and extend a structured orientation to the wiki environment.

- As time goes by, you will be able to share wiki projects from prior semesters with your current students. Create links to published projects that have been made available on the Web and that best represent your expectations for collaboration and quality.

BUILDING THE FRAMEWORK—DESIGNING THE WIKI PROJECT

With your skills in place, you are ready to start planning and building your wiki project. A successful wiki project will follow a basic instructional design process and will include the following steps:

- Define the wiki project's purpose.
- Classify the wiki project's learning domain.
- Define the wiki project's desired outcomes.
- Frame the wiki.
- Kick off the project.
- Develop group roles and ground rules.
- Determine assessment measures.

Define the Wiki Project's Purpose

As online educators consider the question, "Why wiki?" it is our hope that they will develop an answer that goes well beyond, "Because it is there." Too often we have seen the novelty of a new technology or online tool overshadow its instructional purpose. Before an educator can answer, "Why wiki?" he or she must first answer, "What do I want students to be able to do?" or "What do I want students to gain from this learning experience?" The answers to these questions will guide the project's instructional purpose and provide clear direction to the framework or structure of the wiki. For example, the instructor might answer, "I want students to learn about specific places, events, and historical figures in colonial history, and collaboratively build a class wiki that can be built upon in future semesters." In this case, the primary purpose is to enable students to locate, summarize, and organize information about colonial history in order to gain a deeper understanding of the historical period.

Classify the Wiki Project's Learning Domain

With the purpose of the wiki in mind, the next step is to classify the project and match it to its appropriate domain of learning. Placing the project in a specific domain helps the educator to identify goals, behaviors, and outcomes for the project and select an appropriate wiki frame or project type. Benjamin Bloom's Taxonomy of Learning (Bloom, 1956; Anderson & Krathwohl, 2001) remains a useful approach to classifying learning according to domain. Bloom's domains of learning progress from basic knowledge through the higher-order skills of evaluation and creation. In organizing this book, we have grouped Bloom's six domains into three major categories: Knowledge Construction, Critical Thinking, and Contextual Application. Exhibit 2.1 illustrates this organization and provides examples of typical behaviors within each domain.

Wiki Projects for Knowledge Construction   Wiki projects in this category enable the organization of factual information and the ability to understand meaning. A wiki is an excellent tool for sharing information and building a knowledge base. A wiki project can be framed to track, edit, annotate, elaborate on, and organize information on any given topic. Wikis are well suited to documenting rapidly changing and growing subjects or sets of information. Knowledge construction wikis can range from very simple documents, such as Frequently Asked Questions, to more complex knowledge structures, such

Exhibit 2.1
Wiki Project Categories Based
on Bloom's Taxonomy

Knowledge Construction	Critical Thinking	Contextual Application
Remember	**Analyze**	**Apply**
Define	Investigate	Solve
Describe	Examine	Plan
List	Research	Experiment
Label	Explain	Construct
Understand	**Evaluate**	**Create**
Summarize	Critique	Map
Organize	Evaluate	Design
Interpret	Assess	Compose
Elaborate	Debate	Integrate

as topical encyclopedias (for example, Dinopedia at http://dinosaurs.wikia
.com/wiki/Main_Page). Typical wiki projects in this category include:

- Frequently Asked Questions

- Glossaries

- Summaries

- Class encyclopedias

Wiki Projects for Critical Thinking Wiki projects in this category promote
critical evaluation, judgment, and making choices based on research and reasoned argument. Learning teams can use the wiki frame to brainstorm, gather
research, analyze and solve problems, and create action plans. The wiki supports
users in their need to chunk and organize contributions, conduct peer reviews,
establish document styles and standards, and edit final outcomes. Typical wiki
projects in this category include:

- Case studies

- Debates

- Collaborative research papers
- Online critiques

Wiki Projects for Contextual Application   Wiki projects in this category require students to pull together information, concepts, and theories and apply them to new situations or problems. These projects are much more reliant upon group collaboration, and are generally constructive in nature. The wiki is used as a support structure for every aspect of the group process, from the project's formation to the accomplishment of group goals. Wikis have effectively supported such group projects as team-based design, scripting, and storyboarding (West, Sample, & West, 2007). Wiki projects in this category include:

- Process maps
- Team challenges
- Virtual science labs
- Service learning projects

Define the Wiki Project's Desired Outcomes

Once the purpose and learning domain are clear, the educator can begin to list the specific goals or desired outcomes of the wiki project. The resulting list of outcomes will help to clarify student expectations, drive the selection of assessment measures, and provide a springboard for student contributions. In generating the list of desired outcomes, consider both the direct learning outcomes of the project and the indirect or incidental outcomes.

Objective Learning Outcomes (Direct)   These outcomes answer the question, "What will the students KNOW or be able to DO as a result of this project?" Objective learning outcomes focus on the desired knowledge and skills students will gain from the learning experience. Objective learning outcomes start with an observable and measurable action verb, such as *define, create, evaluate, calculate,* or *compare.* For example, an objective learning outcome of the colonial history project might be for students to be able to list historical figures active during the colonization of the United States.

Metacognitive Outcomes (Indirect)   Metacognitive outcomes answer the questions, "What personal attitudes and abilities might students develop as a result of the project?" or "How will this project develop future learning skills and behaviors?" For example, a metacognitive outcome of the colonial history project might be for students to improve online searching skills and their ability to judge the authority of a resource.

Collaboration Outcomes (Indirect)   Collaboration outcomes answer the question, "What collaboration skills and abilities might students develop as a result of this project?" For example, a collaboration outcome of the colonial history project might be for each group to resolve project challenges and problems as a group, and accept responsibility for solutions.

Frame the Wiki

With the purpose, domain, and outcomes clearly defined, it is now time to start constructing the wiki frame. Also referred to as staging, framing establishes the overall structure of the wiki (Mindel & Verma, 2006). Framing provides a loose shell or outline that students can use as a starting point for the project. The frame also provides cues to the students regarding the desired outcomes and organization of the project. Framing helps to eliminate the "blank page" syndrome, and has been shown to encourage earlier and more frequent participation in the wiki (Mindel & Verma, 2006).

Some wiki frames are created within a single wiki page. Most, however, split content into a number of hyperlinked wiki pages. A typical wiki frame includes a home page, content pages, and team process pages. Scaffolding, or pre-populating content, may also be appropriate, depending on the levels and needs of students.

Home Page   At minimum, the wiki frame should include a home page with an introduction to the purpose and goals of the wiki project. It might also include a menu or table of contents with links to content pages, links to team profiles, or guidelines for contributors. Exhibit 2.2 provides a sample frame for the home page of the colonial history class project.

Content Pages   In most wikis, you have a choice of building the empty content pages or using page stubs (indicators for pages to be developed) on the home page. The advantage of page stubs is that students can delete and add stubs before they begin to work on specific pages. It is usually helpful to have at least one sample content page created as part of the wiki frame. The sample page can provide a title and sample structure for organizing content. If you want all of

---

Exhibit 2.2
Sample Home Page

U.S. Colonial History Wiki Project

Purpose: This wiki will provide students of HIST 105 with the opportunity to explore specific places, events, and historical figures in U.S. colonial history. Students will work in teams to collaboratively locate, summarize, and organize information on colonial history in order to gain a deeper understanding of the historical period.

   About This Wiki Project: To learn more about this project, follow these links:

- Goals and Outcomes

- Assessment Measures

- Guidelines for Teams

Table of Contents	Fall 2008 Teams
Early Setters	Team A
Spanish Colonies	Team B
New France	Team C
The British Colonies-New England	Team D
The British Colonies-Middle Colonies	Team E
The British Colonies-Lower South	
The French and Indian War	
The Acts of the Revolutionary War	
Events Leading to the Revolutionary War	

---

the pages in the wiki to have a similar layout and format, you might also include samples and guidelines for font size and color, and for the consistent placement of pictures and tables.

Team Process Pages   If the wiki will be built by collaborative teams, the wiki frame should also provide a space in which the teams can plan, brainstorm, communicate, and practice. Team process pages might include icebreakers, group planning pages, and profiles. Specific tips for managing these pages will be further discussed later in this chapter.

Scaffolding   Scaffolding is a teaching strategy developed by social constructivists to describe the types of assistance offered by an instructor to support learning. A scaffold, or support structure, is provided to students until they are capable of self-directed learning (see Larkin, 2002; Bruner, 1975; Vygotsky, 1978). In a wiki, a scaffold is an extension of the frame and provides a temporary or starting support structure to be used by learners until they self-organize and construct or modify their own knowledge. A wiki frame can be pre-populated with organizational headings and initial content adjusted to the needs of the project and the level of student ability. The level of scaffolding in the wiki will depend on the domain, the desired outcomes, and the current capabilities of the students. Exhibit 2.3 provides a sample content page with scaffolded headings and content.

Exhibit 2.3
Sample Content Page with Scaffolding

U.S. Colonial History Wiki Project: Early Settlers (1526–1565)

Introduction

Explain and provide examples of why settlers chose to colonize in the United States during this historical period. Where did they choose to settle and why?

Colonial Life

What was life like for the colonists?

Time Line

Create a page to explain each key event, colony, or historical figure during this period. Connect each page to a date or time period, and place it along the time line. For example:

1526 – San Miguel de Guadalupe

Resources

Provide a list of resources used for this page.

Kick Off the Project

It is now time to invite students to collaborate in the wiki. Gaining agreement and co-planning the remainder of the project's boundaries are critical to the transfer of ownership from instructor to students. Students will need an opportunity to "claim" the wiki as their own collaborative learning environment, in which they can exert control and begin the process of self-organization.

Provide a team planning area in the wiki, in which students can begin to self organize. This area will support the team's need to plan, assign roles and tasks, and track progress. Ask students to generate a list of products, pages, or deliverables to be developed within the wiki, along with predicted completion dates. Provide feedback concerning the feasibility of the team's project approach and confirm the expected deadlines.

Develop Group Roles and Ground Rules

For newly formed groups, it is important to provide space and opportunity for teams to discuss and define roles and norms. A role can be defined as the tasks and behaviors expected of each team member by other members in the group (Johnson & Johnson, 2006). Roles tend to define the formal structure of a group and differentiate one position from another. For example, a wiki project team might assign roles to a researcher, communication liaison, format editor, and grammar editor, with all team members sharing the roles of writer and text editor.

Ask each student to answer the question, "What will be my role(s) on this project?" Provide feedback to ensure that roles are fair and well balanced. For a successful wiki project, role assignments should be balanced appropriately to ensure that the project goals will be achieved, and should reflect the talents and interests of each team member. Roles should also be kept flexible, so team members can trade and refine responsibilities if the wiki project shifts in scope and direction.

Norms are rules, explicit or implied, established by the group to guide the behavior of all members (Johnson & Johnson, 2006). In a wiki, norms are represented by agreements about wiki etiquette. Although the project facilitator can suggest these rules, only team members can confirm and adopt them as standards of behavior.

Ask students to review and discuss a list of suggestions for wiki etiquette, and then create a list of ground rules for their own teams. Pete Babb of Infoworld (2007) suggests the following ten commandments for wiki etiquette:

- Thou shall not confuse thy opinion with gospel truth.
- Thou shall not invoke personal attacks.
- Thou shall stick to the subject at hand.
- Thou shall cite thy references.
- Thou shall punctuate and capitalize.
- Thou shall own up to thy mistakes.
- Thou shall not use aliases or sock puppets.
- Thou shall not "feed the trolls." (That is to say, thou shall not pick a fight.)
- Thou shall resize thy images.
- Thou shall respect the old adage: What happens on the wiki stays on the wiki.

Determine Assessment Measures

Finally, it is essential to determine how students and teams will be graded and assessed for their wiki accomplishments. How the project is assessed can affect the level and quality of contributions, as well as students' overall satisfaction with the wiki as a learning environment. In summarizing thirteen case studies of wiki projects in a higher education setting, Mindel and Verma (2006) found that "students were significantly more inclined to participate with the wiki when such use was . . . backed up by an explicit assessment or grading scheme" (p. 12). Assessment should consider the following:

- What will be assessed
- Who will be assessed
- Who will participate in the assessment

What to Assess   In considering what to assess, the instructor should begin by revisiting the outcomes defined during initial planning. Revisit the desired outcomes, discussed earlier in this chapter, for objective learning, indirect and metacognitive learning, and collaboration. How will each of these outcomes be measured? What specific criteria will be used to assess these outcomes? Will the focus of the assessment be on the wiki deliverables alone, or will it also include an assessment of each group's collaboration or project management?

Rubrics can be extremely helpful in guiding outcomes-based assessments and clarifying assessment criteria. A rubric is a scoring tool that lists the criteria against which the work will be evaluated. The instructor or group members can construct rubrics using online templates and tools, such as RubiStar (http://rubistar.4teachers.org), or using tools in the online learning management system, if they are available. Constructing rubrics and making them available early in a project help groups to focus their tasks, measure their own progress, and strive for higher levels of quality. Exhibits 2.4, 2.5, and 2.6 provide sample rubrics for assessing both the process and the outcomes of a wiki project.

Exhibit 2.4
Wiki Collaboration—First Group Process Check

Criteria	Exemplary	Above Average	Average	Below Average
Preparedness	All group members have accessed the wiki practice page and have resolved all connectivity and browser issues.	All group members have accessed the wiki practice page, but some have not resolved connectivity and browser issues.	Some group members have accessed the wiki practice page and resolved connectivity and browser issues.	None of the group members have accessed the wiki practice page or resolved connectivity and browser issues.
Openness	All group members display a positive attitude toward online group collaboration and alternative approaches to learning.	All group members display a positive attitude toward group collaboration, but some members display resistance to alternative approaches to learning.	Some group members display a negative attitude toward online group collaboration and alternative approaches to learning.	None of the group members display a positive attitude toward online group collaboration or alternative approaches to learning.

Criteria	Exemplary	Above Average	Average	Below Average
Group Timeline	Group independently develops a reasonable, complete timeline describing project deliverables and completion dates. All students in the group can independently answer questions about the timeline.	Group independently develops a timeline describing most deliverables and completion dates. All students in the group can independently answer questions about the timeline.	Group independently develops a timeline describing most deliverables and completion dates. Most students in the group can independently answer questions about the timeline.	Group needs instructor assistance to develop a timeline and/or several students in the group cannot independently answer questions about the timeline.
Roles	Each student in the group can clearly explain what tasks need to be completed by the group, what his/her role(s) are, and what contribution he/she is making toward group goals.	Each student in the group can clearly explain what tasks need to be completed by the group, but some students are unclear regarding their roles.	Each student in the group can, with minimal prompting, explain most tasks needing to be completed by the group, but none of the students can identify their individual roles.	One or more students in the group cannot clearly explain what tasks are needed by the group to reach goals.

Exhibit 2.5
Wiki Collaboration—Second Group Process Check

Criteria	Exemplary	Above Average	Average	Below Average
Prewriting Activities	All group members consistently engage in brainstorming, outlining, discussion, and other prewriting activities in the wiki.	All group members engage in some discussion or other prewriting activities in the wiki.	Some group members engage in discussion or other prewriting activities in the wiki.	There is no evidence that group members have completed prewriting activities in the wiki.
Integrity of Contributions	All group members are working toward the completion of project goals, making informed contributions, and fulfilling agreed-upon roles.	All group members are working toward the completion of project goals, but some members are falling behind in fulfilling agreed-upon roles.	Most group members are working toward the completion of project goals, but some members are not making contributions.	Few group members are working toward the completion of project goals.
Self-Organization	Group members actively seek feedback from each other, resolve project challenges and problems as a group, and accept group responsibility for solutions.	Group members seek feedback from each other and attempt to resolve project challenges and problems, but will sometimes rely on a single member or the instructor to make decisions.	Group members work independently, but then seek problem resolution, confirmation, or approval from a single member or the instructor.	Group members work independently and do not seek feedback, confirmation, or approval from others.

Exhibit 2.6
Wiki Collaboration—Project Outcomes

Criteria	Exemplary	Above Average	Average	Below Average
Constructive Process	All group members made frequent and constructive additions and revisions to elaborate, refine, and improve the project outcomes.	All group members made occasional constructive additions and revisions to elaborate, refine, and improve the project outcomes.	Most group members made some constructive additions and revisions to elaborate, refine, and improve the project outcomes.	Most group members made constructive additions, but few attempts were made to make revisions to refine, improve, and elaborate on the project outcomes.
Balanced Contributions	All group members worked to complete project goals and fulfilled agreed-upon roles.	All group members worked to complete project goals, but some members had to step in and complete tasks and roles originally assigned to another to meet project deadlines.	All group members worked to complete project goals, but some members' tasks were not complete by the project deadline.	One or more group members did not work toward the completion of project goals.

(Continued)

Exhibit 2.6 *(Continued)*

Criteria	Exemplary	Above Average	Average	Below Average
Organization	All wiki entries are clearly written and well organized, with pages, sidebar content, and links that are easy to navigate.	Most wiki entries are clearly written and well organized, with pages, sidebar content, and links that are easy to navigate.	Most wiki entries are clearly written and organized, but pages, sidebar content, and links are difficult to navigate.	Most wiki entries are clearly written, but are not well organized. Wiki pages are difficult to locate and navigate.
Cohesion	The final wiki project demonstrates outstanding cohesion and consistency in concept, organization, style, and format.	The final wiki project demonstrates outstanding cohesion and consistency in concept and organization, but has some inconsistencies in style and format.	The final wiki project demonstrates some cohesion but has a number of inconsistencies in concept, organization, style, and format.	The final wiki project lacks cohesion and has several inconsistencies in concept, organization, style, and format.

Whom to Assess   You must also consider who will be assessed. Will you assess individual members or the group as a whole? In our experience, it is important to have a balance of assessment measures that can provide feedback to both the individual and the team. For example, drafts and final wiki deliverables can be assessed at the group level, whereas contributions, specific roles, and collaboration outcomes can be assessed at both the individual and group levels.

Who Will Participate in the Assessment?   Palloff and Pratt (2005) suggest that collaborative activities, such as wiki projects, are best assessed through collaboration (p. 44). This means that the instructor should not be the only participant in the assessment of a collaborative project. Self-assessment and peer or team assessments can add alternate viewpoints and provide deeper insights into individual and team achievements. Teams can complete the same rubric(s) used by the instructor to offer a comparative point of view. Peer assessments can be structured to assess how well each group member fulfilled his or her role(s) and met the expectations of the team. Self-assessments offer opportunities for reflection, and can take the form of narratives, rubrics, or questionnaires. Triangulating these measures offers both the instructor and team members a more complete and valid assessment of the project.

MONITORING CONSTRUCTION—MANAGING THE WIKI PROCESS

Okay . . . you've done your planning. Your students are prepared. You focused on the learning context, and the wiki frame is built and posted. You're off to the races. But what if the students don't participate? Fail to self-organize? Experience conflicts? According to Neidorf (2006), "[Online] learning communities face the same challenges as other kinds of communities: conflict, personality clashes, warring agendas, differing work ethics, cultural missteps, and more. Add to these the difficulty of working across time zones and with technology that puts many of us at a communication disadvantage, and it may sometimes seem easier to just forget the entire thing" (p. 171).

It helps to recognize that online collaborative writing is a process. Like any process, it will go through ups and downs. Smoothing out the bumps will require monitoring, management, and facilitation. Don't assume, however, that process management is the sole responsibility of the online instructor. Process management is the primary responsibility of each student group. The role of the instructor is to step in when self-management fails.

It also helps to recognize that wiki groups, no matter how well prepared, will struggle at different stages of the process. As an instructor, know that this not only is to be expected but is actually conducive to meaningful learning. As groups struggle and solve problems, they gain confidence, build collaboration skills, and strive for higher levels of performance. Every group, whether online or meeting face-to-face, experiences stages of group development (Tuckman & Jensen, 1977; Johnson & Johnson, 2006). Early stages of development are characterized by uncertainty and a period of "testing" the rules, procedures, and wiki environment. It is during this stage that group members build trust and put the foundations for productivity into place.

As fears are dispelled and students become more comfortable with their assigned task, the wiki environment, and the roles of group members, the group builds momentum and experiences a surge of productivity. Rewarded by early accomplishments, productivity continues until the group encounters obstacles. Common obstacles include unbalanced participation and group members' not fulfilling their roles and commitments. It is also during this stage that groups experience the positive outcomes of risk taking, creativity, and innovation.

As deadlines near and stress increases, personal conflicts also tend to emerge. Group members may try to exert power and influence over components of the wiki project, and in the process may intentionally or unintentionally attack or diminish the work of another member. It may be necessary to intervene in order to help group members resolve conflict and resume productivity. Helping group members to recall and respect agreements about constructive editing and wiki etiquette will also be important during this stage.

Finally, process management includes the ability to bring a wiki project to the fulfillment of its goals and to provide a satisfying closure to the group. It is often difficult to know when a wiki project is complete. At the conclusion of the project, the instructor helps students recognize their progress and self-assess the quality of the wiki outcomes. On the following pages, we offer additional tips for helping students manage the wiki process through each of these stages.

Creating an Atmosphere of Trust

In the beginning, there is fear. Fear and mistrust are natural reactions to the unknown and the unfamiliar. As your students consider the wiki project, they will very likely express their fears and concerns. Are your students afraid of working in teams? Afraid of an unreliable Internet connection? Afraid of conflict? Afraid of the deadline? Robin Neidorf (2006) believes that online students need an opportunity to express their fears early in the process: "I let them complain. If I don't, they never get over it" (p. 172).

Discuss Concerns   Help students know that they are not alone in their fears. Engage students early on in an open chat or threaded discussion so that they may air questions and issues of concern. Help them realize that most people come into their first wiki project with the same or similar fears. Also let them know that none of the apparent obstacles they express are insurmountable. Balance the negatives with a consideration of the positives and the possibilities. We have found that it often helps to provide students with examples of what real-world teams accomplish through wikis. (For ideas, see the additional resources provided for many of the wiki frames in Chapters Three through Five.)

Build Confidence   It will also be important for groups to build a level of confidence in the wiki technology and trust in their own collaborative skills and abilities. Students must believe that the project goals are reachable and that the tools provided will support them in their work. Only after group members build self-confidence in the wiki will groups be able to build momentum and trust in each other.

Online icebreakers and trial runs are excellent exercises in trust and confidence building. They establish the presence of individuals and serve to open lines of communication (Conrad & Donaldson, 2004). Icebreakers present individuals with an opportunity to enter the learning environment, and to "break the ice" through self-disclosure. Small, non-threatening trial runs in the wiki can also serve as exercises in trust, helping students build confidence in the wiki technology. Exhibit 2.7 provides a sample trial run and icebreaker activity, which can be embedded at the start of a wiki project.

Building Momentum

As the wiki project begins, groups will form relationships and begin the process of collaborative writing. Instructors will find that students often struggle to "make the first mark" in the wiki. A blank wiki, like a blank canvas, can be a pretty intimidating thing. Like many online collaborative activities, early participation and initial contributions can often set the tone for the project. The key is to get students into the wiki and working on productive and meaningful tasks from the beginning.

To help members overcome initial hesitation and move them more quickly into collaborative work, it is essential to provide wiki frames to support the group planning process and to stimulate the collaborative writing. As discussed earlier in this chapter, framing helps to establish the purpose and structure of the wiki project, and provides hooks on which groups can begin to hang their contributions. Although each wiki project will vary in the level and type of structure necessary in the wiki frame, the following are some key ideas to consider during the early phases to help students build momentum.

Exhibit 2.7
Sample Trust Exercises

Sample Trial Run Activity: "Wiki-Libs"	Sample Icebreaker Activity: Stem Statements
Purpose	**Purpose**
To provide the whole class with a fun, interactive trial run to experience logging in and editing in a wiki.	To provide an opportunity for students to share something about themselves by adding to another student's writing in a wiki.
Frame	**Frame**
1. *Word List.* On this page, provide a numbered list. Make sure there is at least one number for each student in the class. For each number, ask the student to provide a word that will replace a word in a text passage. The sillier, the better. For example:	1. *Stems.* Create a wiki page with the heading "Stem … Statements" and the following instructions:

1. Michael (number):

2. Susan (noun, plural):

2. *Text Passage*. Wait to release this page until after students have completed the word list above.

On this page, copy a passage of text that is relevant to your course content or that is very familiar to students. Remove words from the passage that match the word types on the assigned word list. For example:

Four score and (1. number)
(2. noun, plural) ago . . .

MANAGEMENT TIPS
Ask students to log on and provide their assigned word on the word list. This is a simple task that confirms that students are able to log in and find the wiki.

After the word list is complete, release the text passage. Have students log in again and edit the text passage, substituting their words for the numbered locations in the passage. What emerges is often a very comical revision of a famous passage.

"Please post the beginning of a sentence that you would like another student in this class to complete. These statements will help us get to know each other and get familiar with the wiki. Put your name at the beginning of the stem so we know who is writing. For example:

(Katie) My favorite musical group is . . .
(Craig) I am taking this class because . . ."

2. *Statements*. After all of the stems are posted, change the instructions to the following:

"Please complete one of these stems (but not your own!) with an ending to make it a complete statement. Put your name at the end of the statement so we know who is answering. For example:

(Katie) My favorite musical group is . . . U2 (Paul).

(Craig) I am taking this class because . . . I really like online classes (Emily)."

Electronic Courtship   Once the ice is broken and groups are confident in the wiki, groups will need to develop and maintain a high level of trust among their members. Group members can establish trust through a series of early interactions, sometimes called electronic courtship, and through open discussion of roles, ground rules, and expectations.

Make sure that teams have multiple channels of communication available within and outside the wiki. Encourage teams to utilize the built-in discussion areas available in many wikis or to establish a group threaded discussion area in the online learning management system. Be careful, however, not to let groups get mired in discussion and put off their collaborative writing tasks. As a faculty colleague put it, "Just because group members are sharing a work space doesn't mean they are collaborating. Make sure the wiki project isn't all talk and no walk."

Group Planning Pages   As we suggested earlier in this chapter, you can help build momentum by inviting students into the wiki project planning. We typically assign a group planning page as the first task that each group completes during the wiki project. Working on the plan is a low-risk collaborative task that allows group members to get familiar with one another, as well as gain some commitment to, and ownership of, the project goals, deliverables, and timelines.

Profile Pages   To personalize the wiki project, and to sustain individual group members' needs to disclose preferences and work styles, profile pages can be added and hyperlinked from the group planning page. Each team member contributes a single personal page, on which he or she can post a picture and short introduction, as well as disclose role preferences, talents, limitations, links, and contact information.

Prewriting   Like most writing tasks, collaborative writing typically begins with a phase of brainstorming (University of Victoria Distance Education Services, 2007) or prewriting (Peha, 2002; University of Maryland, 2008). Prewriting is the process of organizing thoughts and ideas before beginning to write. Prewriting takes on many different forms, including diagrams or webs, brainstormed lists, lists of key resources, and outlines. Encourage students to engage in prewriting within the wiki. Let them know that early wiki contributions do not need to be perfect examples of writing. Discourage prewriting and drafting in word processing programs outside of the wiki. The advantage of the wiki as a shared workspace is that group members can, and should, collaborate throughout the process. Every wiki will go through an "ugly duckling" stage before it moves through drafting, revising, and constructive editing.

Encouraging Self-Organization

After prewriting, groups enter a phase of increased productivity, adding to and elaborating on content, and developing new pages at a rapid pace. The wiki swells in size and number of entries. Groups often need to be reminded, however, that quantity is not all that is sought in a collaborative wiki project. To be a meaningful learning activity, the wiki project will strive for cohesion, quality, and innovation. As one faculty member put it, "The wiki should be more than a patchwork quilt of text and graphics that results from a divide-and-conquer writing approach." The wiki should represent true collaboration and result in a whole that is greater, and more innovative, than the sum of its parts.

To accomplish this, groups need to occasionally step out of the wiki project's tasks and engage in exercises of reflection and evaluation. It is this seamless movement between action and reflection that results in self-organization. As groups engage in seeking behaviors, reflection, and adaptation, their outcomes become distinct, unique, and self-organized. "To be self-organizing, a living system is aware of, and constantly receives feedback from its environment. This feedback allows the living system to make adjustments that preserve its essential identity" (Johnson, 2002, p. 35). Johnson further suggests that there are five key behaviors inherent in self-organized learning:

- Taking action
- Asking questions
- Developing self-awareness
- Making choices
- Collaborating

Encourage Seeking Behaviors To be successful, learners need to ask interesting, stimulating questions. Encourage students to engage in seeking behaviors, not only asking difficult questions but also seeking out and finding the answers. In a wiki, this might take the form of "What if … ?", "How … ?", and "Why … ?" questions. For example:

- What if we added a page to address this topic?
- What if we reorganized the topics in a new order?
- How have other groups (companies, organizations) answered this question?
- Are there other ways of solving this problem?

Students may address these questions directly to you as the instructor. They may even invite you to edit the contents of their wiki. Instead of answering the questions directly, however, lead the group to online resources, materials, or key experts that might help answer the question. The cardinal rule for the wiki instructor is: Never Edit Their Page! Feel free to comment, but always maintain the group's ownership of the wiki contents and outcomes.

Self-Awareness and Reflection Reflection is not something online students tend to engage in naturally. Students immersed in a wiki project may need some prompting to step out and reflect. Given this assumption, we have learned to build a reflection component into our wiki projects. Reflections can take many forms, including journals, blogs, and weekly reports. Whatever the form, we have found that reflection activities offer individual group members an opportunity to share personal insights, concerns, and questions, which often get lost in the collaborative space. These reflections help students to process the meaning of both the content and the collaborative group process.

Challenging Groups Another key factor in group self-organization is the availability of feedback from the environment. The online faculty member's primary role in this phase is to provide the feedback that will challenge groups and lead them to make choices and adaptations. Feedback can be formal or informal. Formal feedback might be represented by a midpoint assessment of the project, supported by a rubric. Groups typically respond more readily to informal feedback. Periodically asking a group, "What do you see as the strengths of your project?" or "What are your next steps and why?" opens the door to an informal evaluation of the group's process and outcomes. Within these exchanges, watch for opportunities to challenge the students to move to the next step. You might say to them, for example, "You have made great strides in organizing your topics. However, some of your entries are brief. To what areas are you planning to add more detail?"

Constructive Editing

Students are often familiar and comfortable with making constructive comments and contributing to peer evaluations. Many hesitate, however, when it comes to actually making constructive edits to another student's work. They may ask, will my fellow group member be upset if I change his or her wording, or if I reorganize the page? In our experience, students are generally open and accepting of edits to their work if these are made in a constructive manner. So what is constructive, and what is unconstructive, in a wiki?

Stewart Mader, in his book, *Wikipatterns* (2008), identifies several behaviors that can be deemed as unconstructive in a wiki:

- *Do-it-all.* This person tries to control the organization of the wiki and attempts to claim sections of the wiki, blocking others out of his or her "domain."

- *OverOrganizer.* This person spends all of his or her time reorganizing what others have done, without making substantial contributions.

- *WikiTroll.* This person makes negative comments throughout the wiki, without actually making any improvements or changes.

- *Wikiphobe.* This person often suggests that other tools (such as discussions, e-mail, or word processing programs) be used instead of the wiki to complete project tasks.

- *Empty Pager.* This person creates empty pages without headings or structure, expecting others to complete them.

- *Lockdown Manager.* This person exerts control over the wiki by actually locking others out of the editing.

The goal for wiki group members is to engage in constructive editing. Constructive editing is aimed at improving the wiki outcomes while also maintaining collaboration and group cohesion. Edits are made to benefit the group and to move the wiki project forward. Constructive editing becomes easier for students when they trust in the integrity of other team members. Exhibit 2.8 summarizes constructive and unconstructive editing behaviors in a wiki.

Exhibit 2.8

Constructive and Unconstructive Editing Behaviors

Constructive Editing Behaviors	Unconstructive Editing Behaviors
Adding	Protecting or locking text or pages
Elaborating	Deleting passages without comment or reason
Refining	Adding bias
Clarifying	Exerting control or claiming owner-ship over a page or passage
Organizing	Making changes anonymously
Synthesizing	Waiting for others to make substantive contributions
Validating and confirming accuracy	Adding inaccurate or poorly researched passages
Citing and providing references	
Making language consistent and parallel	
Making formatting consistent	

Ensuring a Balance of Contributions

One challenge every collaborative group faces is keeping the workload fair and balanced. We've all been there. A group member, for whatever reason, doesn't pull his or her weight, and the other members have to pick up the slack to prevent the project's failure. According to Palloff and Pratt (2005), "The greatest complaint about collaborative work from both instructors and students is the uneven participation of group members" (p. 10). The amount of effort each group member provides cannot be fully controlled, nor can student emergencies be completely avoided; however, there are some specific steps the online instructor can take to ensure balanced contributions within wiki groups.

Monitoring   A real advantage of a wiki as a teaching tool is its transparency. Almost all wiki tools offer group members and owners the ability to monitor contributions and review the wiki history. The mere fact that students know that the instructor is able to view which, and how many, students accessed the wiki, and when revisions were made, increases the likelihood that each group member will contribute. In monitoring the wiki, look for links to the editing or revisions history and explore these questions:

- How many revisions (versions) have been made?
- How substantial is each revision?
- What is the time span between revisions?
- Which students are making the majority and minority of revisions?

Process Checks   It is helpful to provide process checks at agreed-upon milestones or benchmarks in the project. A process check is an opportunity for all wiki members to step back and assess how things are going. Process checks can be either informal or part of the overall graded assessment of the project. Like the planning page, the process checks can be completed within the wiki. Process check questions might include:

- What is going well?
- How is the team currently collaborating?
- If the group continues with its current process, will it achieve the project goals?
- If not, what should be changed to ensure success?

Individual Assessment Strategies   Another strategy we have used with success is to integrate an individual midpoint assessment. The goal of the assessment is to gauge each individual member's level of familiarity and engagement with the wiki project. The assessment is built as a short-answer quiz in the learning management system, which each member completes privately and independently. The assessment typically reveals the group members who have contributed minimally to a project or are struggling with their roles. Questions on the quiz might include:

- What are the objectives of your wiki project?
- What is your role on the project?
- Based on your group's work plan, what tasks are you responsible for?

- By what date will these tasks need to be completed in order to meet group objectives?
- What knowledge or skills will be required to complete these tasks?

Recognizing and Resolving Conflicts (or Dealing with the Sticky Wikis)

As stress builds and deadlines loom, the group will inevitably encounter conflicts and obstacles (sticky wikis) that slow down the process. According to Johnson and Johnson (2006), a conflict exists when one group member attempts to draw attention to his or her own needs and wants while blocking, interfering with, or injuring another member. The conflicts themselves are not destructive. It is in how they are managed that creates constructive or destructive outcomes. Destructively managed conflicts result in group ineffectiveness, sabotaged work, delays, anger, and apathy. If managed constructively, however, conflict can result in a renewed common understanding, group resolve to solve the problem, adapted roles, and commitment to change.

We have been lucky to encounter few real conflicts in our wiki projects. We credit most of this to the preventative measures already described in this chapter, which were designed to help to monitor projects, provide feedback, and balance contributions. When conflict has come up, however, we have been successful with the following strategies.

Reassess Group Goals and Roles   Most often, conflict arises because team members are not "on the same page" (literally). We see this when wiki groups start out with a divide-and-conquer strategy, and then experience difficulty when they try to come back together and work as a cohesive team. Essentially, these groups expect to be able to bypass the collaborative prewriting and drafting stages, and experience conflict when each member tries to enforce his or her personal agenda in the wiki. If this occurs, ask groups to step back and reevaluate the goals and work plan they outlined at the beginning of the project. It may be the case that because of discovery of new information and the efforts of group members, the goals of the project need to be adjusted or refined. Alternatively, the group may discover that they need to renew commitment to the existing plan. Have the group come to an agreement on the revised project goals and adjust role assignments as needed. At this point, a group member's stepping into the role of style editor or citation checker may help move the project forward.

Controversy Versus Conflict   Help groups recognize the difference between controversy and conflict. Controversy occurs when two pieces of contrasting information in the wiki must be reconciled. Controversy is a positive aspect of problem solving and should be handled through group discussion, negotiation, and consensus. Conflict only occurs when the discussion fails and translates into destructive behaviors. Encourage students to use the wiki tools to address and resolve areas of controversy. Remind students to use the wiki commenting or discussion features to bring attention to inconsistencies, and to ask for suggestions from other group members. We have also found that it helps to highlight passages that need resolution or negotiation in a different color, or to adopt a notation scheme. We further suggest that group members post a comment whenever a substantial edit is made in the wiki. This alerts other team members that the edit was made with integrity and not out of malice.

Wiki Conflict Interventions   In rare cases, you may need to schedule a conflict intervention. If this is required, we highly recommend the use of such synchronous tools as chat or Voice over Internet Protocol (VoIP) conferencing to engage the group members in an open discussion. Because both the synchronous tools and the wiki are available on the Web, invite members to have the wiki and the chat or conference open concurrently during the session. Offer each group member an opportunity to express the problem. Ask students to point to specific pages or passages in the wiki to illustrate the problem. Lead members to small areas of agreement and common understanding. Ask, for example, "Can you each name one thing that is going well in the wiki?" Ask for suggested solutions from each member, and lead the group toward the next steps or action plans. Ask the group to provide a follow-up report (typically, an e-mail is fine) a few days after the session to describe the group's progress and any remaining conflicts.

Conclusion and Closure

Although wiki projects have the potential to live on forever on the Web, the groups that collaborate around them will eventually conclude their work together and continue on their separate ways. If all has gone well, the group's goals and objectives will have been achieved, and there will be pride and a sense of accomplishment in the project outcomes. The conclusion of a wiki collaboration project can be rich in meaning and learning. As an instructor, mine this opportunity to help students make connections, reflect, and integrate what they have learned through the wiki project with their prior learning experiences.

Publishing as a Final Step   Most educational wiki projects begin as private wikis with a defined group of collaborators. Many of these projects result in rich information sources, which can have tremendous value if shared with the global Web community. Encourage groups to plan for, and complete, a publishing step toward the end of their project. In most wikis, this can be accomplished simply by changing permissions or performing a "publish to URL" step (such as with Google Docs, http://docs.google.com). Publishing, as part of the writing process, validates the learning activity, extends the life of the project, and gives group members a sense of pride.

Reflect on the Wiki Experience   According to Johnson and Johnson (2006), groups need an opportunity to bring the project to a close in a satisfying manner. These authors further suggest that closure, or termination, address four areas: completing unfinished business, remembering positive group experiences, reflecting on what each group member has gained from the experience, and expressing feelings about terminating the group. Engage students in a final threaded discussion or synchronous chat aimed at addressing these questions:

- What unresolved issues remain for your group?
- What stands out as a significant learning experience (an "aha" moment) for your group?
- What are you most pleased with in your final wiki project?
- What have you gained as an individual from this experience?
- What advice would you give to next semester's wiki groups as they begin a similar project?
- What final message would you like to express to your fellow group members?

SUMMARY

Although wikis are useful, easy-to-learn, collaborative environments, simply making a wiki available to students is not enough. Successful wiki integration requires preparation, planning, and management. Prepare students for wiki work by helping them understand what a wiki is, and by orienting them to the new learning environment. Include trial runs and icebreakers in the wiki to gain trust and familiarity. Wiki projects can take on many forms and can be framed to support different domains of learning, including knowledge construction, critical thinking, and contextual application. Framing and scaffolding wiki content can facilitate and direct group collaboration, and can lead to more positive learning outcomes. Like all collaborative group projects, wiki projects move through phases that require specific facilitation and management techniques. Once wiki groups have established trust, they engage in planning, prewriting, and self-organization. During the process, online instructors guide from the side, monitoring the project's momentum, ensuring balanced contributions, supporting conflict resolution, and encouraging reflection. In the end, wiki group members experience rich learning and growth as collaborators and members of the online community.

Wiki Projects for Knowledge Construction

Many online courses include learning outcomes that expect students to acquire a fundamental understanding of a subject, field, or discipline. Particularly in general education courses, such as history and science, students must build an adequate knowledge base in order to develop advanced skills in the discipline, think critically, and solve problems. This knowledge base is typically made up of factual information, as well as concrete and abstract concepts. On Bloom's Taxonomy (Bloom, 1956; Anderson & Krathwohl, 2001), these outcomes are best represented by the domains of Remembering (for example, listing, defining, labeling) and Understanding (for example, summarizing, organizing, interpreting).

Historically, teaching strategies that support recall and understanding have emphasized reading, studying, and testing. Durable knowledge construction, however, requires more than reading and rehearsal (Knowlton, 2001). In order for students to transform new information into knowledge, they must actively assimilate the new information with prior learning (Piaget, 1970; Bruner, 1990).

According to social constructivists, knowledge construction is not passive, but active and collaborative (Knowlton, 2001). Learners construct new ideas or concepts by negotiating meaning through social interaction and by connecting new experiences to existing cognitive structures, which are also called schema or mental models (Bruner, 1990). To promote knowledge construction, online activities must

Exhibit 3.1
Wiki Projects for Knowledge Construction

Remembering	Understanding
Resource bank	Annotated bibliography
Frequently Asked Questions	Online dialogue
Error finding and correcting	Group summary
Historical time line	Class encyclopedia

provide students with opportunities to actively collect and organize information, and to collaboratively transform that information into cognitive structures.

Wiki projects in this chapter are designed to enable knowledge construction. A wiki is an ideal environment for online students to share and organize information, and negotiate the meaning of new concepts. A wiki project can be framed to help students list, define, elaborate, edit, annotate, summarize, organize, and elaborate on information from nearly any subject or discipline. Wiki projects in this chapter range from very simple documents, such as Frequently Asked Questions, to more complex knowledge structures, such as class encyclopedias. Specific projects are listed in Exhibit 3.1.

RESOURCE BANK

There are many different collaborative wiki projects that you can use in an online class. Where do you start? It can be easier to begin with wiki projects that have fairly simple tasks, such as brainstorming ideas or creating a list of links (Lamb, 2004). A resource bank is a good first wiki project to try with novice students. Although this type of project could also be accomplished in a blog or a discussion forum, learners in these environments have little control over how resources are organized, and are not able to edit or add to existing lists. A resource bank may provide the flexibility and dynamic nature students are seeking.

Purpose

Using a wiki as a resource bank allows learners to add and modify information centering on a specific topic. The wiki gives learners the freedom to organize and present the information on the topic in ways that are more meaningful to them. A resource bank wiki can be used in a number of different ways:

- Create a list of Web links related to the course or topic. Ask students to post their favorite Web sites or online resources. (For a more detailed assignment, see the discussion of annotated bibliographies later in this chapter.)

- Use the wiki for file management and sharing. A wiki is a great place to upload and share files. Depending on the wiki, files can be hyperlinked or attached, and can range from Microsoft Word or PowerPoint files to images and media files. Whereas other Web services, such as e-mail, offer the ability to share files, the wiki places in the hands of the learners the power to add to and organize the files. It also allows for the addition of annotations or file descriptions.

- Create a contact list. A wiki can serve as a database of information about people or places. The wiki allows learners to share, modify, and edit information that others may have posted. For example, a wiki can be used as a central location for identifying U.S., state, and local legislators. It also allows learners to post more detailed information and hyperlinks about the contacts.

Frame

Home Page   A resource bank wiki will, at least, need a home page. Use this page to provide directions on what types of information are appropriate for the wiki and suggestions for organization. Provide one sample posting as a guide or model.

Category Pages   In most cases, your students will naturally add new pages or categories to the wiki to organize resources. When a list of links gets long, encourage students to divide the list into multiple pages. In some cases, it may be helpful to set up major category pages for students in advance. For example, in a list of information about U.S. national parks, you may want to create separate pages for the different regions of the United States.

Management Tips

- Encourage collaboration by having students edit or clarify entries. It is useful to use a discussion or comments area for posting explanations and the reasoning behind changes and edits.

- If you are using the wiki to upload and organize files, make sure you provide guidelines as to what file types are acceptable. For example, with digital images, JPG and GIF files are usually wiki-friendly, whereas proprietary software files, such as Photoshop files, are not.

- It may also be necessary to limit the size of the file to be uploaded. This is especially important if you are using a free wiki service with limited storage capacity.

FREQUENTLY ASKED QUESTIONS

A Frequently Asked Questions (FAQ) document seeks to provide answers to questions commonly asked in regard to a particular topic, concept, or process. Traditionally, questions have been generated by users or students and collected by an instructor or moderator. The instructor must then write the answers to the questions and distribute them, either online or in a printed document. With a wiki, students have the ability to ask the questions, answer them, or both. Frequently Asked Questions are often found on Web sites and in software documentation.

Purpose

A Frequently Asked Questions wiki project can serve as an effective study aid for small or large groups. It can be helpful as a means for learners to share with the rest of the group both the questions they have concerning a particular topic and their knowledge and understanding. FAQs are useful projects when the desired learning outcomes are to share perspectives and strengthen understanding of a topic or discipline. FAQs can be used to answer such questions as:

- Where do I find information on . . . ?
- How do you . . . ?
- How would you solve . . . ?
- What is significant about . . . ?

The instructor can set the parameters for the types of questions that will be included in the FAQ. Students may add their own questions within the guidelines, or answer questions that have been provided by the instructor. The wiki allows for multiple perspectives and for one student's ability to elaborate on another student's answer. For example, one student may supply the name of a resource and another may provide the hyperlink or contact information.

Creating the FAQ in a wiki allows students the freedom to organize and rearrange questions and answers. For example, in one online course, students were asked to create a FAQ that would help future students. After several questions had been posted and answers provided, one student divided the page into two categories: one for students interested in taking the course and one for students once they had enrolled. Students eventually organized the FAQ into more specific categories as more questions were added. Figure 3.1 shows a sample FAQ page created by students using a wiki.

Figure 3.1
Frequently Asked Questions Wiki

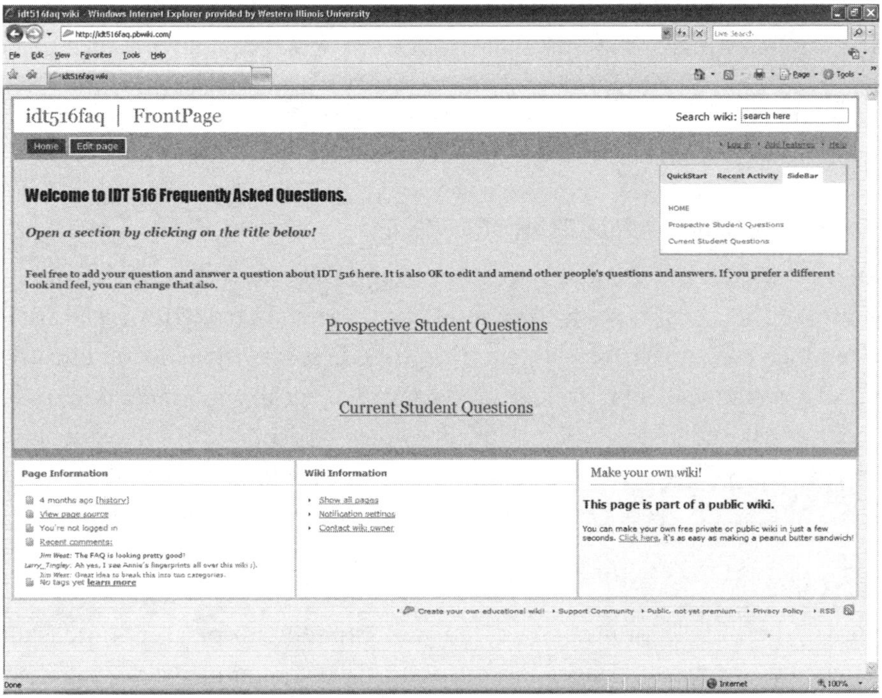

Source: http://idt516faq.pbwiki.com/

Frame

FAQ Page   Generally, a FAQ can be started with just a single wiki page. Provide minimal scaffolding on the page, including a descriptive title and a hyperlink to guidelines regarding acceptable questions and answers. Provide a sample question with an answer that meets these expectations.

Management Tips

- Provide guidelines for adding and answering questions. Do you want students to add their own questions, or will you provide the questions yourself? Generally, learners will be capable of both adding and answering questions in the wiki. A good rule of thumb is to require each student to ask at least one question and answer at least one question asked by someone else.

- Wikis are meant for collaboration. Encourage students to verify one another's responses and edit or clarify them if necessary. It is useful to use a discussion or comments area to post explanations of, and the reasoning behind, changes and edits.

- If someone posts a question that no one answers, provide guidance to help someone answer the question. For example, "Consider checking out Source A to answer this question."

ERROR FINDING AND CORRECTING

Wikis are an ideal medium for projects involving collaborative review and editing. A wiki project that requires students to locate and correct factual errors can promote recall and serve as an effective study aid. This works best when you include intentional errors in a narrative, list of facts, or study questions. It encourages students to read the material closely and to use the wiki editing features to identify and correct the errors. This type of project is a good way to introduce learners to the collaborative editing process, and can be very effective in promoting teamwork and collaboration.

Purpose

Use this type of wiki project when you want students to be able to determine the accuracy or validity of factual information. This type of activity is particularly appropriate for the disciplines of math, science, social science, and information technologies. Depending on the topic, this project can be used for small or medium-sized groups.

Frame

Home Page   Use the home page to provide directions and set expectations. The instructions need to include information about what students should look for on the page and how to make corrections. Provide hyperlinks to the drafts to be corrected and edited.

Drafts   The draft pages will contain the materials that the students will review and correct. If you are working with small groups, you will need at least one draft per group. For each draft, provide one to two pages of text related to the topic being studied. Populate the page with intentional errors. These might include misspelled places or names, false facts, or erroneous definitions. Depending on your topic, students may need to research the subject or review their textbooks to determine the accuracy of the information provided.

Hints and Resources   Create a page with accurate and reliable resources on the topic. For example, if the students will be reviewing the draft for historical accuracy, include links to time lines and reliable Web sites to help them determine what dates and time periods are correct.

Management Tips

- Most wiki tools can easily support this type of activity. If you are creating a project for multiple groups, however, you may need a wiki service that allows you to control access to specific pages within the wiki (usually not available with free wiki services). An alternative is to eliminate the home page and set up a separate wiki for each group. Provide the assignment directions at the top of each group's draft page or in the online course materials.

- You will need a bank of content that can be edited or corrected. If you will be using a copyrighted text, ensure that you are within the rules of fair use for education or obtain permission from the author.

- This activity can be modified for a variety of disciplines. You can, for example, ask students to identify errors in computer code, maps, design documents, or statistical analyses.

- Monitor the page and provide a running total of errors that the students have not yet found. For example, "Great job . . . only three errors left!"

Additional Resources

- Wikipatterns: Intentional Errors. Available at www.wikipatterns.com/display/wikipatterns/Intentional+Error.

HISTORICAL TIME LINE

In many disciplines it is important for students to gain a sense of the historical significance of individual events that may have shaped the current field of study. It can be difficult for students to study these events without understanding the relationships of the events to other events or current practice. Placing these events on a continuum or time line can help students to gain a better sense of the historical period in question and the impact each event may have had on the field. Historical time lines are a staple of education and have been built in a variety of text and Web forms (see, for example, Sass, 2008; Nothiger, 2008).

Purpose

Before wikis, Web-based time lines had to be managed and assembled by a single Web developer. The wiki allows for time lines to be built through collaboration and peer review, enabling a more robust and useful teaching tool in a shorter period of time. Students can construct historical time lines as a private team project or as a public wiki project. Creating an historical time line is effective when your desired learning outcomes include historical research and analysis skills, and when you need your students to discuss the historical significance of particular people or events.

Frame

Time Line The main wiki page provides the historical period on a visual time line, usually built vertically down the left of the page. The time line is broken into years or months, depending on the overall period being studied. Individual events on the time line are represented by title and date, and are hyperlinked to individual event pages. If you are assigning particular events to groups or students, you can indicate this as part of the event title. Although most time lines use formatted text, graphics can also be added to the event hyperlinks to increase the visual appeal and impact of the time line. Figure 3.2 shows an example of a historical time line wiki.

Figure 3.2
Sample Time Line Wiki

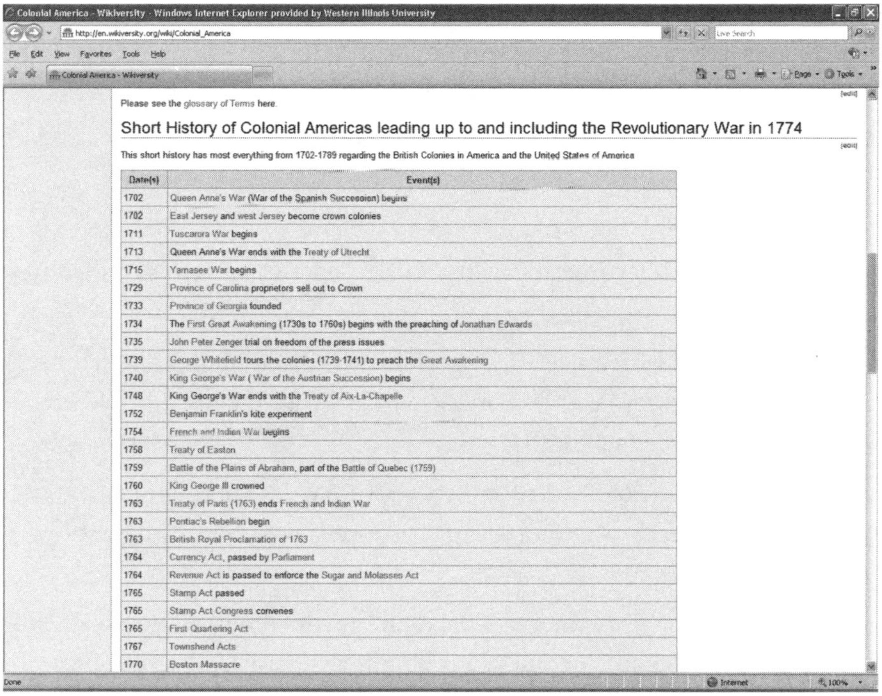
Colonial America - Wikiversity - Windows Internet Explorer provided by Western Illinois University

http://en.wikiversity.org/wiki/Colonial_America

Please see the glossary of Terms here.

Short History of Colonial Americas leading up to and including the Revolutionary War in 1774

This short history has most everything from 1702-1789 regarding the British Colonies in America and the United States of America

Date(s)	Event(s)
1702	Queen Anne's War (War of the Spanish Succession) begins
1702	East Jersey and west Jersey become crown colonies
1711	Tuscarora War begins
1713	Queen Anne's War ends with the Treaty of Utrecht
1715	Yamasee War begins
1729	Province of Carolina proprietors sell out to Crown
1733	Province of Georgia founded
1734	The First Great Awakening (1730s to 1760s) begins with the preaching of Jonathan Edwards
1735	John Peter Zenger trial on freedom of the press issues
1739	George Whitefield tours the colonies (1739-1741) to preach the Great Awakening
1740	King George's War (War of the Austrian Succession) begins
1748	King George's War ends with the Treaty of Aix-La-Chapelle
1752	Benjamin Franklin's kite experiment
1754	French and Indian War begins
1758	Treaty of Easton
1759	Battle of the Plains of Abraham, part of the Battle of Quebec (1759)
1760	King George III crowned
1763	Treaty of Paris (1763) ends French and Indian War
1763	Pontiac's Rebellion begin
1763	British Royal Proclamation of 1763
1764	Currency Act, passed by Parliament
1764	Revenue Act is passed to enforce the Sugar and Molasses Act
1765	Stamp Act passed
1765	Stamp Act Congress convenes
1765	First Quartering Act
1767	Townshend Acts
1770	Boston Massacre

Source: http://en.wikiversity.org/wiki/Colonial_America

Individual Event Pages Students or groups become responsible for the construction of each individual event on a new wiki page. Encourage students to thoroughly research their event and to provide citations and resources to support their findings. Keep event pages relatively brief and encourage the inclusion of hyperlinks to additional sources of information. Encourage students to include graphics and maps, if these will help the reader to visualize the historical significance of the event. Depending on the level of consistency you hope to see in each page, you may wish to provide a sample completed event with the headings you wish to be included. For example:

- Title, Date, and Location of the Event
- Description

- Significance
- Resources

Guidelines for Contributors   If you are building the time line as a public wiki, be sure to include a page with guidelines for authors and contributors. Invite contributors to peer review and edit existing pages or to add events to the time line. Identify rules for editing and wiki etiquette.

Management Tips

- Integrate a peer review into the wiki project. This can be accomplished in several ways:
  - Match students with a peer throughout the project. Identify benchmarks at which a peer review will be completed (for example, during research, the first draft, and the final draft).
  - Invite an outside expert to review the event pages. Use the threaded discussion related to each page as a means to support comments, suggestions, and author responses.
  - Ask students to review the event pages in the time line and post a minimum number of comments or questions about the historical significance of the events to the pages' threaded discussions. Follow the review with a synthesis discussion of the key concepts that the students identified. This can be done in the wiki or learning management system.
- Consider keeping the wiki project private until the initial drafts are completed. At that point, make the project public. Students often step up the quality of the project when they know it will have real usefulness to others outside of the course.
- Rather than starting from scratch, consider organizing your time line project so that it adds to an existing public wiki, such as Wikiversity's Social Science Portal at http://en.wikiversity.org/wiki/Portal:Social_Sciences.

Additional Resources

- Hopkins, G. (2005). Timelines. *Education World.* Available at www.education-world.com/a_curr/strategy/strategy033.shtml.

ANNOTATED BIBLIOGRAPHY

An annotated bibliography is an alphabetical list of resources, usually containing a citation and a description of the source. The bibliography can relate to almost any subject. Depending on the topic, the annotated bibliography usually works best with smaller groups. The items in the bibliography can be any type of resource. Web bibliographies, or "Webographies," are annotated bibliographies of Web sites.

Purpose

Annotated bibliographies, or Webographies, are more than just a list of articles or links with brief descriptions (see the discussion of resource bank wikis earlier in this chapter). Annotations often include, in addition to descriptive information, an assessment of the value of the resource. An annotated bibliography has the potential to inform readers of the appropriate audience for, and the overall scope and usefulness of, each resource. Use an annotated bibliography project when your desired learning outcomes include information searching and evaluation skills, and when you are looking for ways to support the exploration of readings and resources beyond your course textbook.

Because annotations can vary widely, it is important for the instructor to clearly state what should be included in each annotation. There are different types of annotations, depending on the learning goals of your project (University of Michigan, 2004). Basic annotations describe the central goal or purpose of the resource, and generally include a brief description of the content and the overall scope, audience, or purpose of the resource. More informative annotations will expand on basic information and include a summary of the contents, key ideas, and conclusions of the sources. Even more detailed annotations incorporate the student's evaluation of the value of the resource, including its important strengths and weaknesses. These three types of annotations are known as:

- Indicative

- Informative

- Evaluative

A wiki allows students to pool resources in a comprehensive, annotated bibliography. The quality of the bibliography will depend on the process and skills students use in searching for, locating, and selecting resources. Small groups can collaborate, helping each other with search strategies and in evaluating the resources to be included in the project.

Frame

Home Page   At the very least, an annotated bibliography wiki project should have a home page that describes the scope of the project and provides links to assigned topics. Provide clear guidelines and expectations for annotations on the home page, or link to a separate style guide.

Group Topics   The number of additional wiki pages will depend on the number of groups and the topics to be assigned. Each group should have its own page for constructing its annotations. For each group page, include the assigned topic and list of group members at the top of the page.

Style Guide   Finally, you should include a page with your expectations, sample annotations, and links to available resources for helping learners complete the assignment. Guidelines should include what information is expected in each annotation and the preferred format or style to be used. Link to a style manual (APA, MLA, etc.) or on-campus style guide that is appropriate to your discipline. Consider including tips or resources for online searching as well. See Exhibit 3.2 for sample annotations.

Exhibit 3.2
Sample Annotations

Sample Web resource annotation (Indicative, Generic Style)

Illinois Virtual Campus

www.ivc.illinois.edu/

An extensive list of distance education courses and programs from seventy-two Illinois colleges and universities, ranging from two-year associate degrees to doctoral degrees. A clearinghouse of information for the distance learning student.

Sample print resource annotation (Informative, APA Style)

Harroff, P. A., & Valentine, T. (2006). Dimensions of quality in Web-based adult education. *American Journal of Distance Education*, 20(1), 7–22.

This article reports on a study concerned with understanding program quality in Web-based adult education. The authors gathered information about program quality from administrators and educators at five national and regional conferences. The article identifies six dimensions of program quality in Web-based adult education. It reports that quality of instruction, one dimension, relies on quality of interactions, quality of materials, and quality of technology used. The second dimension involves quality of administrative recognition and support. This involves instructor support in several areas. The quality of advisement is the third dimension, and involves what Web-based students receive from organizations. The fourth dimension, the quality of technical support, concerns the technical support and technology required to train instructors. The fifth dimension of quality involves providing information for potential students about such topics as admission procedures, hardware and software requirements, and financial aid. The final dimension addresses the quality indicators for evaluation of the program, course, and facilitator. The study also addresses access to Web-based adult education for students with learning and physical disabilities, and finds that access to instruction is limited for these individuals in many Web-based education programs. The article reports on the actual results that were discovered by the use of the instrument designed by the researchers, and compares them to results found in previous studies. The article also utilizes a secondary analysis to provide deeper understanding in the area of administrative recognition, and in the different perspectives of various staff providing technical support. The article concludes with recommendations for future research.

Sample print resource annotation (Evaluative, APA Style)

Minkel, W. (2003). Dollars for development. *School Library Journal,* 49(9), 54–55.

This article outlines the effects of President Bush's No Child Left Behind (NCLB) legislation on teacher training and development, and on the way schools are working to comply with these requirements under current budget restraints. The article quotes Joan Vandervelde, director of online professional development at the University of Northern Iowa. Dr. Vandervelde gives information about, and examples of, technology used to deliver professional development courses, and provides lists of federal grants available to schools. The article talks about how NCLB dictates that teachers be highly qualified and trained. It gives information on how that is being done through online courses, noting how schools in Iowa follow up this training with the use of such technology as e-mail, Iowa Communications Network (ICN), and videoconferencing. The article was useful and provided some good information, particularly in regard to grant possibilities for professional development in the areas of technology and other subjects.

Management Tips

- This activity works best with small groups of three to six people. The whole class can be involved, however, by regrouping and organizing annotations into a single page once they are constructed. Another option is to ask students to review and comment on at least one other student's annotation, either in the wiki or in a related discussion forum.

- This type of wiki project can help students learn the publication styles for your discipline. Encourage students to "style-check" each other's annotations and ask questions about proper citation methods.

Additional Resources

- Assignment Assistant: Annotated Bibliography. Available at www.lib.umich.edu/ugl/guides/assist/assignments/annotatedbib.html.

- Writing an Annotated Bibliography. Available at www.utoronto.ca/writing/annotatebib.html.

ONLINE DIALOGUE

Another quick and easy way to incorporate wikis into your online course is to have students conduct small group dialogues. The dialogue can take the form of a role play or informal debate, with each group taking a different character or choosing a side in an issue. Although a discussion forum is often used for this type of dialogue, a discussion does not easily support the construction of a cohesive and shared response. The wiki allows groups to collaboratively construct, edit, and refine a shared contribution before the other group picks up the dialogue. Further, this type of activity allows students to take the time to research their character or position, and to frame a response that is thoughtful and appropriate to the conversation.

Frame

Home Page The home page should describe the central theme, situation, or issue for the activity. The page should also provide general guidelines concerning when and how each group should post. For example, if the dialogue is to discuss two sides of an issue, you might organize the dialogue sequence as:

- Teams A, B, C – Construct "pro" arguments by Monday, June 8.
- Teams D, E, F – Construct "con" arguments by Monday, June 15.
- Teams A, B, C – Draft responses by Monday, June 22.
- Teams D, E, F – Draft responses by Monday, June 29.

Team Dialogue Pages Match teams from each side of the issue (Team A with Team D), or teams that represent the characters to be role-played, and give each pairing a shared dialogue page. Provide the guiding question, issue, or theme at the top of the page. Include headings on the page that indicate where each stage of the dialogue should be written.

Management Tips

- This wiki activity works best with groups of two to five students. You will want to identify multiple themes or topics, with separate dialogues for each. It will be useful to build these topics around a central idea or theme.

- Give each group a certain number of days to frame their responses before the opposing group responds. Explain to the students that once the next group begins to add its part of the dialogue, the previous portions of the dialogue should not be changed. Instead, students will need to wait until it is their turn to add to the dialogue to clarify or explain their remarks.

GROUP SUMMARY

Summaries written by small groups are good candidates for wiki projects. Students in small groups can review relevant course materials and write their summaries directly into a wiki page. Summaries can be written based on a wide variety of readings or written materials, and are appropriate for all subjects and disciplines.

Purpose

A written summary is an effective tool to gauge student comprehension of a particular reading or resource. It allows students to express key concepts and ideas in their own words, and to explain their understanding of the materials they have reviewed. This type of wiki project emphasizes facts and concepts, and puts less emphasis on analysis and evaluation than do the critical thinking projects found in Chapter Four. The completed group summaries can serve as study aids for the rest of the class. Students can complete summaries on a variety of written material, such as:

- Textbook chapters or units: What are the main ideas and key points?
- Literature (novels, short stories, plays, etc.): What is the story about? Who are the main characters?
- Geography (for example, country reports): What type of government does the country have? What are the main industries? What is the climate like?
- Business (for example, company reports): What products does the company produce? Who are the corporate officers?

Frame

Table of Contents   Provide an organizational page for the wiki, outlining the readings, chapters, or businesses to be summarized. If readings will be assigned to groups, indicate readings next to each chapter or topic.

Summary Pages   Each group should have its own wiki page on which students can write their summaries. If the summary must cover particular questions or issues, scaffold the page with leading questions or subheadings. For example, a chapter summary might include the following subheadings:

- Central Idea
- Key Concepts
- Facts to Remember

Management Tips

- Assign summaries to groups of no more than three to five people.
- Set up each summary page as private to its assigned group during the early stages of the project. After the groups have completed their summaries, you can then make the pages public or share access with the rest of the class.

CLASS ENCYCLOPEDIA

Collaboratively writing a class encyclopedia is a great way to use a wiki with a large group of students. In fact, depending on the topic and scope, this type of project can involve students across multiple courses and multiple semesters.

Each semester, new learners can have the opportunity to add to the encyclopedia and review existing entries.

Purpose

The purpose of a class encyclopedia is to collaboratively build a rich resource that represents students' collective intelligence in regard to a particular subject. This subject can be very broad (for example, world history), or more narrowly focused (for cxample, types of mammals living in North America). Very specific topics based on a single person or event (for example, The Gettysburg Address) are generally too narrow in scope for a large group encyclopedia project.

It will be essential to select the right wiki service for this type of wiki project. Encyclopedia projects require a wiki that can support multiple pages and the organization of entries. It is important to select a wiki service that allows your students the freedom to build the encyclopedia effectively and efficiently. Some things to consider include:

- The number of pages you can create
- The ability to link between pages
- Users' ability to search for pages

This might seem to suggest that only self-hosted wikis (such as MediaWiki or TWiki) can adequately handle this type of project. However, many wiki services can be used for this type of project—even free wikis—if framed properly. Framing is an essential step in preparing students for adding and editing entries in a class encyclopedia.

Frame

Home Page   This page should provide a brief overview of the wiki, its purpose, and its goals. The home page should also include a menu with links to main articles and to a page providing guidelines to contributors. To help users browse through the contents of the encyclopedia, it can also be useful to provide links to selected featured articles or new entries.

Article Pages   Each article or entry in the encyclopedia should have its own page on the wiki. Articles are linked to additional articles through embedded wiki links. Provide scaffolding for the article pages to include suggested subheadings and page stubs, which are hyperlinks that lead to new, empty articles and are meant to encourage users to add additional content related to the subject.

Guidelines for Contributors The guidelines should help students understand the depth and format expected for articles. You should also include suggestions for constructive editing, including guidelines for wiki etiquette. Because most encyclopedias include pictures and other media, provide guidelines for adding these types of files to entries. Particularly if the wiki is a public project, include compliance and copyright guidelines relevant to posting content, images, and media.

Management Tips

- This activity is appropriate for groups of all sizes, and works well with very large groups.

- You will need to determine how to assign articles in the encyclopedia. Do you want individuals contributing or do you want small groups to work together?

- You can either set up pages for the main articles that learners should complete (for example, with page stubs) or allow learners to add their own articles. If students add their own articles, encourage them to always provide a hyperlink to the new page from an existing article. This avoids "widowed" or lost articles.

- Make sure your wiki service allows users to upload images and other media files.

- You will need to refer to your school's copyright and compliance procedures, perhaps including a link to your campus policy on the page containing contributor guidelines.

Additional Resources

- Copyright on the web. Available at http://webdesign.about.com/od/copyright/a/aa081700a.htm.

- Copyright and web teaching. Available at http://www.dartmouth.edu./~webteach/articles/copyright.html.

SUMMARY

There are a wide variety of wiki projects that can be used effectively in an online class. Where do you start? It can be easier to begin with wiki projects that have fairly simple tasks and knowledge-based learning outcomes. Wiki projects for knowledge construction can usually be created using any wiki service, whether you are using a wiki tool in your learning management system or a free service like WetPaint. Wiki projects that focus on knowledge construction can engage large classroom groups (for example, Frequently Asked Questions or class encyclopedias) or small groups (for example, online dialogues or group summaries). Using a wiki for collaborative knowledge construction gives learners control over content organization and encourages students to develop a shared understanding of facts and concepts. Wiki project frames should provide an appropriate amount of structure for students to accomplish project goals and fulfill the desired knowledge outcomes. In the next chapter, we will focus on wiki projects that promote evaluation and critical thinking.

Wiki Projects for Critical Thinking

Critical thinking is currently a key issue in the reformation of higher education. According to a recent report from the Association of American Colleges and Universities (AACU, 2007), critical thinking stands at the center of essential learning outcomes "that all students need from higher learning [and] that are closely calibrated with the challenges of a complex and volatile world" (p. 2). Critical thinking skills cut across all subjects and disciplines, and enable students to thoughtfully consider, critically evaluate, and apply reasoned judgment to problems. Facione and Facione assert, "Critical thinking comes down to reflective decision-making and thoughtful problem-solving about what to do or what to believe" (2007, p. 40). On Bloom's Taxonomy (Bloom, 1956; Anderson & Krathwohl, 2001), critical thinking is represented by the domains of Analyzing (for example, examining, researching, investigating) and Evaluating (for example, interpreting, critiquing, evaluating).

Educators have employed a wide variety of instructional strategies to promote critical thinking, with a recent emphasis on critical writing, guided inquiry, and collaborative learning activities (Bean, 2001). Online, these strategies are most

---
Exhibit 4.1
Wiki Projects for Critical Thinking

Analyzing	Evaluating
"What if . . . ?" scenarios	Evaluation or research study
Case studies	Frame-based writing
Debates	Nominal group technique
Collaborative research papers	Structured online critiques

---

often manifested through online discussion, individual writing assignments, and collaborative projects (see, for example, Conrad & Donaldson, 2004; Palloff & Pratt, 2005). Within most online course systems, however, each of these can pose challenges to online students striving to engage in effective critical thinking. Online discussions, for example, support early stages of analysis and elaboration, but it can be difficult to bring the discussion to a conclusion, solution, or group consensus. Online group reports and writing assignments have been burdened by technology limits, which force students to divide the task and forward drafts to members, tracking edits through multiple revisions.

The wiki provides a collaborative work space that can support a wide variety of critical thinking exercises. Wikis are particularly suited to supporting critical writing and group research reporting. A wiki project can be framed to help students brainstorm, research, analyze problems, and collaborate to reach thoughtful solutions and decisions. The wiki supports users' needs to organize ideas, conduct critical reviews, engage group members through comments and questions, and come to a consensus concerning final outcomes. Wiki projects in this chapter range from small case studies to more structured decision-making models. Specific projects are listed in Exhibit 4.1.

"WHAT IF . . . ?" SCENARIOS

Using "What if . . . ?" scenarios is a good way to introduce learners to collaborative critical thinking. You can use any wiki tool to set up these scenarios fairly quickly. The key is to encourage learners to keep asking, "What would happen if . . . ?"

Purpose

"What if . . . ?" scenarios allow learners to review a situation and predict what would be the outcomes or consequences should one or more factors be changed. Rather than reading about and accepting information as it currently stands, learners are expected to analyze a situation's variables and determine the potential impact if the situation, setting, assumptions, or inputs are altered. You can use "What if . . . ?" scenarios in any subject area. For example:

- History: "What if Hitler had not attacked the Soviet Union?"
- Science: "What would happen if you added more heat to a sealed container?"
- Business: "What would happen if I increased the number of salespeople on the floor?"

Frame

Home Page   The home page will serve as a menu or table of contents for scenarios in the wiki. Organize the scenarios on the home page by student groups or by scenario type. Hyperlink to each of the scenario pages you have assigned and include directions and deadlines for completing the scenarios.

Scenario Pages   Each scenario page assigned to a group should contain the scenario details, as well as one or more "What if . . . ?" questions, to which the group will respond. Scenarios should be descriptive and realistic, and should include sufficient details for students to be able to identify variables. If the scenario is based on a current event or news item, link to a Web site or blog entry with additional information. A sample scenario is provided in Exhibit 4.2.

Management Tips

- "What if . . . ?" scenarios are typically most effective in small groups of two to four students. Decide whether all groups should work on a copy of the same scenario or if each group should complete a different scenario.
- This activity requires that students first identify the factors with an impact on the current scenario before they begin writing. Encourage groups to share suggestions and ideas about the scenario in the wiki's discussion or comments area before they work on a written response.

Exhibit 4.2
Sample "What If . . . ?" Scenario

Lisa is the manager of a small retail outfit. The store has a sales force of fourteen people, all of whom are paid on commission. She usually staffs three people during the weekdays and five people on the busier weekend days. The salespeople seem to be pretty busy. She has noticed an increased number of customers coming into the store. However, her sales are flat compared with those of last year. When talking with her staff, she hears several comments that many customers come in, look around, and then leave without buying anything or even talking with a salesperson. Lisa suspects that with the increased number of customers, her staff doesn't have the time to meet and interact with them all.

What would happen if she increased the number of salespeople on the floor?

- Depending on the time available to complete the assignment, respond to students with follow-up questions in the wiki that promote additional thinking. For example, "Did you consider . . . ?" or "Have you also thought about . . . ?"

Additional Resources

- What is Critical Thinking? Learn the Problem-Solving Skills and Make Quality Decisions. Available at www.sinc.sunysb.edu/Stu/sumusso/thinking.htm.

CASE STUDIES

Students use case studies to explore in depth a specific, real-world problem, group, event, or question. Although they are often associated with business and the social sciences, case studies are becoming more common in all areas of study (Pyatt, 2006). Case studies encourage students to evaluate the strengths and limitations of a situation or problem, and to suggest alternative solutions and actions.

Purpose

Select a case study wiki project when your desired learning outcomes are to build situational analysis skills and encourage students to solve problems and find solutions collaboratively. Case study opportunities abound in almost all academic disciplines, providing opportunities for faculty to bring real-world problems into the classroom for analysis. The key to an effective case study is having an open-ended problem or question that may have many different, yet nevertheless valid, answers or solutions. Cases can often be built around current news events, real-world observations, or recently published research.

Frame

Home Page   The home page of the case study should contain an introduction to the case, links to guidelines for completing the case study, relevant case materials, and each group's case solution page(s).

Guidelines for Completing the Case Study   The guidelines need to clearly explain what the groups need to do to complete the case study response or solution. They include guidelines for students to follow when researching, analyzing, and writing their case solutions. If possible, provide an assessment rubric identifying the criteria that will be used to evaluate case responses. (See, for example, the sample rubric in Chapter Two.)

Case Materials Page(s)   Organize supporting case materials on a wiki page with links to relevant news or research articles, data, Web sites, real-world artifacts, and other sources of information, which will inform students' analysis of the case. Supporting case materials generally fall into three categories:

- Artifacts: These are simulated documents that provide evidence and details to enrich the case. The instructor can develop or collect artifacts. For example, if the case study involves a fictional company, you could include a description of the company, biographical information about company principles, financial reports like quarterly statements, and more.

- Analysis aids: These include tools such as survey forms or templates, which the students can use to complete the case study. These materials may consist of several different pages.

- Useful links: Links give students opportunities to engage in deeper research on the case, and can include articles, news feeds, and relevant Web sites.

Case Study Solution Pages   Provide a separate wiki or set of wiki pages in which each group can engage in the case analysis and build a case solution.

For online groups, it is helpful to structure the group wiki to support the research, analysis, and writing phases. This can be done with headings or by constructing separate wiki pages for each of the following phases:

- Research: The research phase involves finding and utilizing resources to gain a complete understanding of the current case. Provide an area in which students can share discoveries and insights regarding the facts of the case. Students may choose to collect information from additional sources, through online searching, interviews, surveys, and other methods.

- Analysis: Once the information has been gathered, learners need to sort through it to determine how best to organize and formulate their understanding of the problem. Provide an area in the wiki where students can brainstorm ideas and engage in problem analysis. To facilitate group discussion during this phase, make sure each group has access to online communication tools, such as chat and discussion forums.

- Writing: The final outcome of the project for each group will be the actual case solution. If the solution must address specific questions, consider scaffolding this page with subheadings or stem statements to guide the organization of the final solution.

Management Tips

- Case studies work best with small groups of three to six people. It is typically most effective for each group to study the same case. This allows for follow-up discussions regarding the diversity or similarity of solutions.

- You can adjust cases to make them more or less difficult. For novice students, provide additional scaffolding by adding helpful resources and case materials, or by periodically releasing "hints."

- Case study projects offer opportunities for students to work with outside experts. Consider bringing in a professional from your discipline to provide insights and feedback concerning students' analyses.

Additional Resources

- NTLF's Frequently Asked Questions (FAQ): Case Studies. Available from the National Teaching and Learning Forum at www.ntlf.com/html/lib/faq/cs-utenn.htm.

DEBATES

Debates allow students to explore opposing sides of an issue by means of a structured dialogue. An organized debate requires students to defend a point of view based on evidence and reasoned arguments. Using a wiki to present a debate allows students to post, edit, and clarify these viewpoints. Students in a wiki debate can add evidence to another student's argument or clarify the language of an argument, which results in a debate that represents students' diverse points of view.

An excellent model for using debates in a wiki is Debatepedia (www.debatepedia .org). This site is designed to allow users to create debates, present arguments for or against a proposition, and provide evidence to support those arguments. For example, a current debate asks, "Should governments be spending resources exploring space?" Debatepedia is a free resource, with which any user can edit responses and contribute to the debate topics.

Purpose

Create or involve students in an online debate when your desired learning outcomes include developing reasoning skills, and when students must:

- Become more familiar with key issues related to a particular topic
- Gain a balanced perspective on a topic
- Express views on a topic that are based on evidence and research
- Critically evaluate opposing sides of an issue

Frame

In framing the debate, allow students to select which position they will support, or divide the class into two groups: one for and one against the proposition of the debate. If needed, you can further divide each side of the debate into smaller groups and assign specific arguments. In preparing for the debate, students will need to research the topic and identify resources that support the point of view they will adopt.

Debate Page The debate can usually take place on a single wiki page. You will need to set up the wiki page with the debate question, background information, and a structure for framing arguments on the two opposing positions. A sample wiki frame might look like the one in Exhibit 4.3. The space exploration debate on Debatepedia is shown in Figure 4.1.

Exhibit 4.3
Sample Debate Wiki

Topic:

Background:

Argument 1

For (Debate in favor of this argument)	Against (Debate opposed to this argument)
References	References

Argument 2

For (Debate in favor of this argument)	Against (Debate opposed to this argument)
References	References

Argument 3

For (Debate in favor of this argument)	Against (Debate opposed to this argument)
References	References

Management Tips

- Instead of populating the debate page with a long list of evidence, consider linking to a new wiki page, on which students can post their evidence, resources, and references.

Figure 4.1
Debatepedia Wiki

Source: International Debate Education Association. Available at http://wiki.idebate.org/index.php/
Debate:Funding_for_space_exploration.

- As the course instructor and facilitator, it is important for you to avoid taking a position during the debate. Instead, focus on the process and on providing feedback to students regarding their reasoning, arguments, and evidence.

Additional Resources

- Debatewise. Available at debatewise.com/.
- Online Teaching Activity Index: Debates. Available at www.ion.illinois.edu/resources/otai/Debate.asp.
- Welcome to Debatepedia. Available at http://wiki.idebate.org/index.php/Welcome_to_Debatepedia%21.

COLLABORATIVE RESEARCH PAPERS

Probably the most common and traditional group writing project is the group research paper or presentation. Collaborative research papers are typically completed by a small group of two to four students, and emphasize research, writing, and collaborative outcomes. In a wiki, students can complete all phases of the research and writing process in a shared workspace. They are able to build off of one another's strengths and create a single, unified writing project.

Purpose

Select this type of project when you want students to research and explore a course-related topic in more depth. Collaborative writing projects can be adapted to almost any discipline and help students develop information literacy and group collaboration skills. Projects can be simple, narrowly focused "white papers" (short discourses designed to educate or inform, which can be completed in a short time frame), or they can be more comprehensive, thorough treatments of an assigned topic.

Frame

It is highly recommended that you provide each collaborative research group with its own, private wiki, which can usually be set up easily with a free service such as pbWiki or Wikispaces. Within each group's wiki, provide pages that support group planning, research, and writing.

Group Planning Page   Establish a page that includes a listing of group members and an area in which students can begin the planning process. Scaffold this page to include early steps in the planning process, with such headings as:

- Research Topic
- Group Member Roles
- Goals
- Outline

Research Page   Provide a page that students can use to track research and highlight key resources. During early research and writing, this page will become a work table, through which students can extract quotes, identify page references, link to relevant Web sites, and share research discoveries. In the final stages of the project, this page will become the list of references used in the paper.

Paper At the center of the project is the paper itself. The framework for this page will evolve as the paper is developed. Encourage students to engage in stages of writing, including outlining, drafting, editing, and refinement. Have students start by converting the high-level outline from the planning stage into headings and subheadings in the paper. Provide adequate time for students to move the paper through the writing process, so that they do not rely on a divide-and-conquer strategy in the wiki. See Figure 4.2 for an example of a collaborative research paper on Copyright that was written in a wiki.

Figure 4.2
Sample Collaborative Research Paper

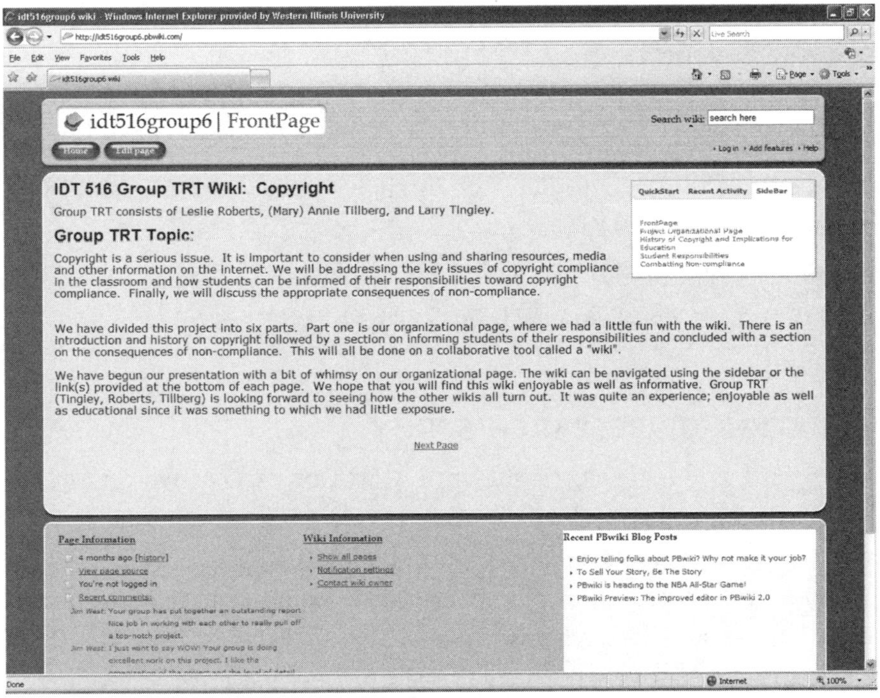

Source: http://idt516group6.pbwiki.com/FrontPage

Management Tips

- If your formatting requirements are high, consider a wiki service that includes advanced formatting features, such as Google Docs.

- It is usually more efficient to assign research topics or provide a selected list of topics from which groups can choose, rather than to leave this choice open-ended. With asynchronous work, it can be inefficient to have groups select a topic, as this discussion can take days or weeks to resolve.

- Discussion forums can play an important role in a collaborative research and writing project. Ensure that students have access to a discussion forum in the wiki or in your learning management system to support group questions, comments, and negotiations.

- This project can easily be adapted to virtual group presentations. Instead of paragraph narratives, encourage students to set up a wiki page for each "slide" in the presentation. Google Presentations, part of Google Docs, also supports collaborative slide-show development.

Additional Resources

- Why Consider Collaborative Writing Assignments? Available at http://wac .colostate.edu/intro/pop2l.cfm.

- Collaborative Writing and Research in Higher Education. Available at www .stanford.edu/group/collaborate/.

- Assigning Collaborative Writing: Tips for Teachers. Available at http:// wrt-howard.syr.edu/Handouts/Tchg.Collab.html.

EVALUATION OR RESEARCH STUDY

Anyone who has ever mentored student research or participated on a research advisory committee knows that the research planning process can be a complex series of negotiations between the student and advisors. Writing in a collaborative space—especially during the research proposal stage and during the development of such research instruments as surveys, evaluation rubrics, and interview questions—can expedite the review process and provide a robust environment for mentoring.

Purpose

Use this approach with individuals or research teams when your desired learning outcomes include the ability to frame research questions, explore the significance of a research topic, and design a research study that includes the use of data collection instruments.

Frame

The framework for the wiki can be based on institutional guidelines for theses and dissertations, or on other guidelines for academic research. Providing a research proposal in a wiki framework can serve as a mentoring tool, and can include references and links to samples, research development tips, and suggestions from the research mentors. See Figure 4.3 for a sample dissertation research proposal in a wiki.

The following structure represents common decision points during research planning:

Table of Contents   Use this page to organize the wiki's planning documents. The page serves as an "advanced organizer" of the research design process and supports the wiki's ability to expand and grow throughout the life of the research project. Include, in addition to hyperlinks to the research planning pages, a link to a page with contact and biographical information concerning the key researchers and mentors.

Research Topic   In the early stages, this page can serve as a sounding board and discussion starter for narrowing the research topic and identifying research questions. As the project progresses, this page will serve as the research proposal's introduction.

Background and Significance   The research team will use this page to justify the significance of the research project and to summarize the related research literature.

Method   This portion of the wiki may be represented by one page or by multiple pages, depending on the level of detail you require in the research proposal. This section will describe the basic research design and methodology, and may

Figure 4.3
Sample Dissertation Research Proposal Wiki

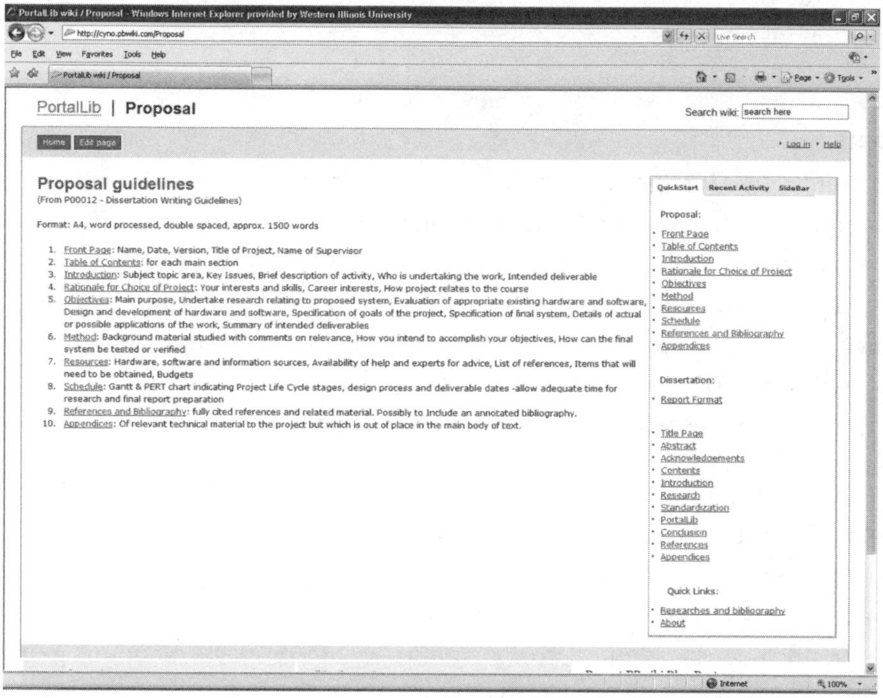

Source: Nicolas Cynobar. Proposal: http://cyno.pbwiki.com/Proposal

include information on research subjects, the research setting, data collection methods, and timelines.

Data Collection Instrument   If the research study includes the creation of a data collection instrument (for example, a survey, interview protocol, observation instrument, or evaluation rubric), consider using the wiki for working through drafts. The wiki's revision history will allow the student and mentors to monitor the evolution of the instrument and restore earlier drafts, if needed.

Resources   Encourage students to construct a wiki page to track the resources they have used throughout the process and in the review of related literature. Divide the page into:

- Cited Sources
- Other Resources
- Suggestions from Mentors

Management Tips

- Choose a wiki tool, such as pbWiki, that supports commenting and gives students the ability to view and restore the document history of each page.

- Work with other research mentors to assemble an agreed-upon wiki template or framework for the research proposal. Use the sidebar in the wiki template to link to departmental samples and writing guides.

- If data collection instruments will be created using tools, such as survey generators, make sure the information can be converted to HTML, Adobe Acrobat PDF, or other file types that can be attached to the wiki page for review.

Additional Resources

- Collaboration in Academia Wiki. Available at http://collaboration.wikia.com/wiki/Category:Academia.

- Academic Publishing Wiki. Available at http://academia.wikia.com/wiki/Main_Page.

FRAME-BASED WRITING

Frame-based writing assignments provide students with a frame or structure that shapes the overall content of a topic the instructor chooses, but leaves gaps in the information for students to complete (Bean, 2001). Students work together to "fill in the blanks" with details, opinions, and supporting arguments. Frame-based writing that promotes critical thinking should emphasize opinion, criticism, and evaluation, and should be more than a fill-in-the-facts exercise.

Purpose

The purpose of frame-based writing is to provide students with a framework or outline that they can use to organize their thoughts and opinions (Nessel & Graham, 2006). The instructor presents the frame, which contains keywords, stems, or critical ideas that students then expand and complete. A frame activity can include many different types of writing:

- Opinions
- Justification
- Comparing and contrasting
- Interpretation
- Persuasion

Frame

Frame-based writing activities work well with small groups. Provide each group with a writing frame, which they will research and complete as a group. Decide whether each group will complete the same frame-based activity or whether you will provide each group with a unique activity.

Home Page Use the home page to give directions and set expectations. Include links to each group's framed activity. Consider including a sample completed frame to help students get a better sense of the format and of your expectations for the depth and clarity of their responses.

Frames You will need a framed wiki page for each group. Construct and copy the writing framework into each group's page. Frames will vary based on the type of activity and the level of scaffolding you provide. See Exhibits 4.4 and 4.5 for sample frames.

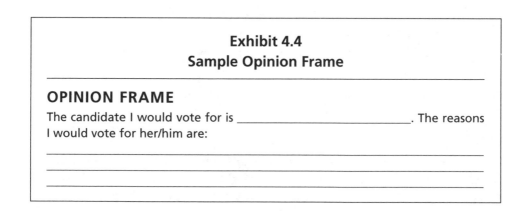

Exhibit 4.4
Sample Opinion Frame

OPINION FRAME

The candidate I would vote for is _____. The reasons I would vote for her/him are:

_____
_____
_____

JUSTIFICATION FRAME

Based on what you have read regarding the automobile industry, what do you think are the reasons for the growth of the Japanese automobile industry and the decline in market share of U.S. automobile corporations? Place your answers in the frame below.

The reasons for the growth of the Japanese automobile industry are several. First, (state your reason and justification). Second, . . . Third, . . .

There are also several reasons for the decline in market share of U.S. automobile companies. First, . . . Second, . . . Third, . . .

Management Tips

- This activity works very well in a shared document wiki, such as Google Docs or Google Presentations. Google documents can easily be copied and shared with a defined group.

- Students will probably brainstorm initial ideas, which will later need to be refined into a cohesive group response. Encourage students to use a color or notation scheme to indicate initial contributions from different members.

NOMINAL GROUP TECHNIQUE

Nominal group technique is a systematic group decision-making method that follows a group through the phases of problem analysis, idea generation, evaluation, and ranking of solutions (Johnson & Johnson, 2006). The technique guarantees that all group members will have the opportunity to participate, and helps guide the group toward an agreement or consensus.

Purpose

Because nominal group technique walks students through a highly structured, prescribed process, it is useful for groups in need of added support to gain consensus, or for groups having difficulty reaching an agreement. This technique can also help minimize the conflict that arises from a controversial question or a problem with a wide variety of answers or solutions. The use of nominal group technique results in a rank-ordered list of the ideas the group members find most suitable or agreeable. It is a useful framework when students must answer questions that begin as follows:

- What is the best . . . ?
- What is the most important . . . ?
- What is the most significant . . . ?
- What are the top reasons . . . ?

Frame

Unlike other wiki frames, in which many of the initial pages are posted at once, this wiki frame is presented in timed phases. Typically, the phases take place within the same wiki page. If you want to track the decision-making process, however, you can create a new wiki page for the discussion and clarification phases (prior to voting) and for the final rankings.

Problem or Question   The problem or question is posted at the top of the wiki page. It is useful to set off the question with a box or horizontal rule so that the question always remains at the top of the page throughout the process. Post the question and, if possible, allow some time for the question to "simmer" before students begin to post ideas.

Idea Generation   Just below the question, post brief instructions for brainstorming their initial ideas. Tell students NOT to edit other students' ideas during this phase. This should be an open brainstorming session in which all ideas are accepted. Push students to be creative, to post multiple ideas, and to build off of the other ideas already posted.

Discussion and Clarification   After students have generated their ideas, you and the group will move into the clarification phase. Expand the area on the page underneath each idea to allow for comments and suggested edits. The goal in this phase is not to eliminate any ideas, but instead to give the students an opportunity to clarify the language and intent of each idea they have posted.

Voting—Round One   In this phase, students will each vote on the ideas they agree with the most, based on the discussion and clarification completed above. To calculate the number of votes each student will have, take the total number of ideas generated and divide by three. This is called the N/3 method. Students vote

Exhibit 4.6
Nominal Group Technique Wiki

What nineteenth- or twentieth-century invention has had the greatest impact on how we live today?

- Telephone

  Comments: The landline phone, not the cell phone.

  Votes: AB, XY

- Calculator

  Comments: Specifically, the handheld scientific calculator.

  Votes:

- Personal Computer

  Comments:

  Votes: CD

- Television

  Comments:

  Votes: AB, CD, XY

by placing their initials or a unique symbol below each of the ideas for which they wish to vote. The instructor or moderator will then tally the votes and post the top vote getters as part of the group's final rankings. Exhibit 4.6 illustrates what the wiki page might look like after the first round of voting.

Voting—Round Two (Optional) If the idea generation phase created a very large number of ideas, or if voting in the first round did not create an obvious list of winners, you may wish to employ two rounds of voting to help narrow the ideas down to a more manageable size. After the first round of voting, eliminate all of the ideas that received zero, or a very small number of, votes. Recalculate the number of votes each student will have in the second round by dividing the total number of votes remaining by three. Erase the first round of votes, and open the voting page as a clean slate.

Final Rankings When the process is complete, create a new wiki page and copy the ideas with the highest votes in rank order.

Management Tips

- Present a fun or simple question the first time you use nominal group technique to get students familiar with the process and at ease with the wiki.

- It may be difficult to judge the time frames required for each phase of using nominal group technique in a wiki. For larger groups, allow twenty-four to forty-eight hours for the idea generation, discussion, and clarification phases. Voting can typically be completed in a single day, with the whole technique requiring no more than a week. For smaller groups, these time frames can be collapsed into single days or even hours.

- Take advantage of colored text, which is typically available in most wiki editors, during the idea generation and voting phases. Assign colors to each member at the start of the process and ask members to do all of their posting, commenting, and voting using their assigned colors.

- As the instructor, be sure to stay neutral during the clarification stage. Help students to maintain control over their ideas and ownership of the resulting rank-ordered list.

STRUCTURED ONLINE CRITIQUES

Structured online critiques give learners the opportunity to critically evaluate a product or material against a set of accepted criteria. Using a standard set of criteria helps learners move beyond subjective responses and provides consistency when comparing one product or material with another.

Purpose

Online critiques go beyond summaries or reviews, which focus mainly on facts. Use structured online critiques when your desired learning outcomes include critical evaluation and formulation of opinions and values, and when students must compare one product or outcome with another. A critique can target almost any product or outcome. Some examples of products to critique include:

- Films, videos, or books
- Advertising or marketing materials
- Research studies

- Web sites or Web applications
- Software products

Frame

Home Page   The home page should include the details of the assignment, as well as links to the evaluation criteria and to each of the group critique pages. Links to completed critiques from prior semesters are also useful. Indicate whether students will be assigned a product to evaluate or whether groups will locate their own products.

Evaluation Criteria   This page should spell out the specific criteria that students will use as they evaluate the product or outcome and prepare to write the critique. This can be a checklist of accepted criteria, a link to an authoritative source, or an actual scoring rubric for the product that each group will complete.

Critiques   Provide a wiki page on which each group will write its critique. It is important for students to know that the final critique should be narrative in form, and present more than a score from the scoring rubric. Based on the evaluation, the final critique should address:

- Strengths
- Limitations
- Conclusions
- Recommendations

Management Tips

- Students may find it difficult to reconcile differences of opinions with other group members when writing the critique. Remind students to base their evaluation on the standard criteria and encourage students to look for specific evidence to support their opinions.
- This project can, over time, result in a useful, comprehensive list of critiques. Consider organizing critiques in a public wiki at the end of the project to benefit a larger Web audience. For example, wikis that collect and share film, book, or educational software critiques would be appropriate as public wikis.

SUMMARY

When framed effectively, wikis can support collaborative projects that promote critical thinking, writing, and problem solving. Critical thinking projects cut across subjects and disciplines, and enable students to analyze problems, critically evaluate outcomes, and apply reasoned judgment to decisions. The wiki provides a collaborative work space that can support the phases of group problem solving and collaborative writing, including research, planning, brainstorming, and developing solutions. Many wiki projects for critical thinking are more appropriate for small groups of two to six members. Instructors should thus select a wiki service that allows users to create private wiki spaces and frames of multiple pages. As groups face the challenges of reconciling differences and writing cohesive responses, instructors must place themselves in the roles of facilitator and cognitive coach. Wiki frames provide the scaffolds and structures necessary to promote organization, logic, and sound reasoning. In the next chapter, we will focus on wiki projects that promote the application of skills in real-world contexts.

Wiki Projects for Contextual Application

As students mature and advance in their learning, it becomes necessary for you to give them opportunities to apply and transfer their developing skills to a variety of new problems and situations. Skills, to be durable, must be portable and transferable outside of the protective walls of the classroom. Learning experiences must encourage students to CREATE and DO, not just think. On Bloom's Taxonomy (Bloom, 1956; Anderson & Krathwohl, 2001), these learning outcomes are best represented by the domains of Applying (for example, experimenting, planning, mapping) and Creating (for example, designing, composing, integrating).

Contextual learning is based on the premise that learning and meaning emerge from the relationship between content and context. It is the context (the environment or problem) that gives meaning to the content (Johnson, 2002). Contextual teaching and learning engage students in significant activities—in rich learning environments—that help them connect their academic learning to real-life situations and problems.

It has always been a challenge for educators to find meaningful ways to bridge the gap between the classroom and the real world. In traditional classrooms,

Exhibit 5.1 Wiki Projects for Contextual Application	
Applying	**Creating**
Event plan	Story creation
Process map	Team challenge
Virtual science lab	Media design project
Field research project	Service learning project

the solution has been to take students out into the world, through field trips and field studies, internship programs, and apprenticeships. Organizing such activities for online students can be difficult, if not impossible. Instead, online educators have learned to capitalize on the world of Web resources to bring the real world into the classroom, by means of well-constructed simulations, virtual team applications, and real-world service projects.

Contextual application projects must be framed to support all phases of group work, from the planning and goal-setting phases to closure and the final evaluation of outcomes. The wiki project should, as much as possible, support self-organization and mirror real-world processes, requiring students to reflect on their perspectives, seek and collect information, and apply a variety of skills to collaboratively design and construct outcomes and solutions. The role of the online instructor in the wiki project is to provide the tools (the wiki), and the context (the problem, artifacts, and guidance) within which this type of activity can occur. Wiki projects in this chapter range from group event planning to more ambitious service learning projects, and represent only a small sample of real-world projects that can be accomplished with the support of a wiki. Specific projects are listed in Exhibit 5.1.

EVENT PLAN

A wiki is especially suited to supporting student groups in the planning of curricular or extra-curricular events. The event could be a mini online conference, panel discussion, mock election, or service learning project. Event planning requires the ability to set an agenda and timelines, and to assign and track the completion of tasks. Event details can change frequently. Building and maintaining a set of shared event documents keeps the entire team aware of each member's progress, and prevents details from slipping through the cracks.

Purpose

An event plan can be a suitable project for small or large virtual teams, especially those that are just forming. Just as in classic movies, when the neighborhood rallies to "put on a show," event plans can bring team members together to accomplish a shared objective. Teams are rewarded with the ability to participate in and evaluate the planned event. Use the event plan when your desired learning outcomes include organization skills, and when you need to foster and build community.

In most cases, the instructor should choose the type of event (and secure any necessary organization approvals) before involving the students or teams. Choose an event that is interesting, but manageable within the time frame of the course.

Frame

Home Page   Structure the home page to include the title, date, and description of the event. Either establish an announcements area on the page or, if available, use the page's threaded discussion to handle news, updates, group decisions, and questions.

Agenda   Use this wiki page to build the detailed agenda, including the titles (what), responsible parties (who), times (when), and locations (where) of each agenda item.

Planning Page(s)   Depending on the scope of the event, this part of the wiki may be represented by a single task list, or may include several pages, with teams taking responsibility for different aspects of the planning. For more complex projects, consider the following planning elements:

- Tasks and timelines (broken into categories if needed)
- Budget and expense tracking
- Marketing and promotion
- Evaluation planning

Management Tips

- If the project requires that you track the budget or expenses, consider using a shared spreadsheet program, such as Google Spreadsheets, part of Google Docs, for this page. "Publish" the spreadsheet to a URL and link to the spreadsheet from your main wiki source.

- Consider holding synchronous online meetings during the planning process on a Voice over Internet Protocol conference call (for example, in Skype) to check on progress and clear obstacles. During the call, have team members document changes and decisions directly in the wiki.

Additional Resources

- MIT Zero Waste Event Planning Guide Wiki. Available at http://openwetware .org/wiki/MIT_ZeroWasteEvent_PlanningGuide_Wiki.

PROCESS MAP

Process mapping is a technique often used by business teams and work groups looking for ways to make a job or process more efficient. A process map uses symbols and arrows to illustrate the flow and impact of current processes, allowing teams to identify problem areas and opportunities for improvement. Process maps have been used in a variety of disciplines, including education, business, agriculture, manufacturing, engineering, and software design.

Purpose

As a wiki project, process mapping offers the virtual team a structured approach to analyzing process-related problems. It is a useful approach when your desired learning outcomes include observation skills, analysis skills, and the ability to see relationships between various processes. Use the process map approach to answer such questions as:

- Why does a process take so much time and require so many steps?

- What types of errors are made in the process? Why?

- Do people involved in the process need better tools, more information, or greater authority to complete the process?

- How can we design the process for the best speed, accuracy, efficiency, and enjoyment?

The instructor can present the process to be analyzed, or the wiki team can select it. Select a process you suspect has redundancies, unnecessary delays, or loops. It is usually easy for students to find and select a process to analyze, as students encounter poorly designed and inefficient processes every day. We have had student teams analyze everything from the process for purchasing an airline ticket online to the process of enrolling in a course. Processes should be current (not historical), accessible, and able to be directly observed by the teams. Help students look for opportunities to interview the people involved in the process in order to gain information about their role in the process. For example, asking, "Why did you do that step?" can reveal additional details about the process.

Constructing the process map in a wiki environment allows team members to aggregate multiple observations of the same process, capture notes and observation details, and present and negotiate ideas for improving the process. The wiki environment makes it easy for teams to share the completed process maps and their suggestions for improvement with decision makers, subject experts, and guests.

Frame

Home Page   The home page should support teams in identifying roles and beginning the dialogue concerning effective and ineffective processes. Consider including:

- Guidelines for constructing a process map: Summarize or link to general guidelines and resources for process mapping. See the additional resources below for suggestions.

- Team roles: Teams should be prepared to identify who will be involved in selecting and describing the process, observing the process, creating the map, editing the map, and identifying opportunities for improvement. In our experiences, it is best if these roles are assigned to multiple group members and not to a single individual. Collaboration should occur throughout the project for greatest benefit.

- Opening discussion: Exhibit 5.2 is an example of a discussion starter, which is useful in raising awareness and jump-starting the brainstorming process:

Process Description and Macro Map   Provide a page on which students can brainstorm and select the process that they will analyze. Once selected, the page can be used to provide an opening description and macro map, or high level overview, of the process.

- Make sure students choose a process that exists today and that the team can directly observe.

- Before creating the process map, students should identify the key inputs and outputs of the process in a macro map. This helps to establish boundaries and keep the team focused on a single process. See Figure 5.1 for a sample macro map.

Process Map   The core of the wiki project is the process map itself. Include sample graphics of the basic symbols for inputs or outputs (ovals), tasks or steps (rectangles), decisions (diamonds), and process flow (arrows), which students can copy and use in their diagrams. Students should map the process from left to right. If the map requires more detail and must extend beyond the edge of the available wiki page, use connector symbols (for example, "A") or hyperlinks to related pages. See Figure 5.2 for a sample process map.

Suggestions for Process Improvement   This page should be structured to allow the team to jot notes and highlight or annotate steps or transactions in the process that are suspected problem areas (for example, time delays, confusing steps, or incomplete transactions). As the project progresses, teams can use this area to brainstorm suggestions for process improvement and to suggest ways the process should be redesigned.

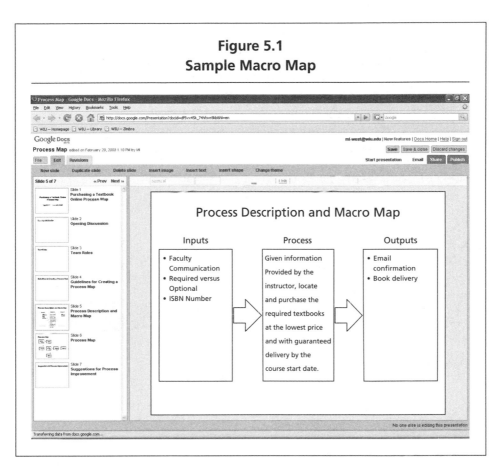

**Figure 5.1
Sample Macro Map**

Management Tips

- Choose a wiki tool that supports graphics and makes it easy to copy, paste, and edit. For example, Google Docs supports the ability to create both documents and presentation pages with inserted images. Images must be in a Web-ready format (for example, GIF or JPG files). Google presentations also support the ability to layer text on top of inserted graphics, making it easy for students to customize their process maps.

- If you are allowing students to select the process to analyze, include a step in the project that requires instructor approval of the process the team has selected. Throw out any processes that are historical in nature (for example, how something was built or invented) and that team members cannot directly experience or observe.

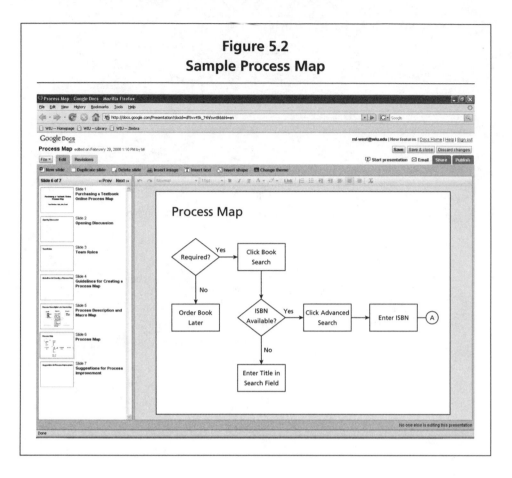

Figure 5.2
Sample Process Map

• Keep each team's wiki private to team members until the process maps are completed. Once completed, have students publish their projects to a public URL or extend access to the remaining members of the class. Ask students to comment on the process improvement suggestions each team made and to offer additional suggestions. This can be accomplished by adding a comments page to each wiki or by linking to the wiki project URLs from a threaded discussion in the online course.

Additional Resources
• How to Map a Process. Available at www.strategosinc.com/process_map_example.htm.

VIRTUAL SCIENCE LAB

Integrating active learning experiences into online science courses can be a real challenge, because scientific inquiry demands observation and experimentation. Wikis open a new avenue of possibilities for integrating virtual lab experiences into online courses. You can ask students and teams to create science labs and experiments (for example, in an online science fair) or to complete virtual labs in wiki lab manuals.

Purpose

Use this approach when your student learning outcomes include following scientific inquiry processes, developing observation skills, and designing and implementing scientific experiments. This approach is particularly useful when you need to promote collaboration among virtual lab teams. Collaborative completion of a virtual lab manual allows team members to compare findings and discuss interpretations of lab observations and results. See Figure 5.3 for an example of a virtual science lab wiki.

Frame

This framework provides a suggested structure for a virtual lab manual.

Table of Contents   Organize and link to the virtual labs from an annotated table of contents that provides the title and description of each lab experience. You can also use this page to make lab team assignments, if teams will complete different lab experiences.

Virtual Lab Pages   The instructor can construct lab pages, with students completing only the lab observations and questions sections. Alternatively, the framework can be used to structure an online science fair, with students or teams completing all sections of the virtual lab. For each lab, provide the following information:

- Introduction
  - Objectives
  - Time required
  - Materials and equipment required

Figure 5.3
DNA Microarray Virtual Lab from Wikiversity

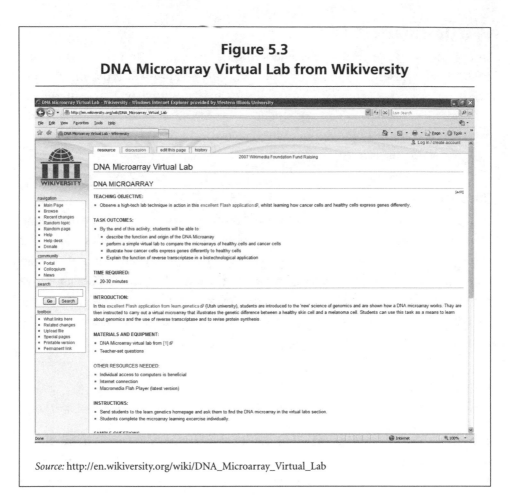

Source: http://en.wikiversity.org/wiki/DNA_Microarray_Virtual_Lab

- Instructions
  - Step-by-step lab instructions
  - Links to online lab resources (interactive multimedia, video, audio, graphics, etc.)
- Lab manual
  - Observations
  - Questions and conclusions
  - Ideas for further investigation

Resources Provide links to useful tools, such as online calculators and virtual lab instruments. Provide guidelines for contributors and sample evaluation rubrics if students will be both designing and completing the virtual lab pages.

Management Tips

- Consider creating virtual labs in a public wiki (for example, Wikibooks (http://en.wikibooks.org) with an accompanying lab manual, which can be completed by students or teams in a private wiki (for example, pbWiki or Google Docs).

- Find and link to labs already available in Wikibooks in your lab manual. Go to http://en.wikibooks.org and type "lab" in the search field.

- Integrate publisher-provided and online multimedia into your virtual lab manuals. Look for resources through some of the following multimedia databases:

  - MERLOT—Multimedia Educational Resource for Learning and Online Teaching. Available at www.merlot.org/merlot/index.htm.

  - TeacherTube Science Channel. Available at www.teachertube.com/channel_detail.php?chid=59.

  - The University of Virginia Virtual Lab. Available at http://virlab.virginia.edu/VL/home.htm/state=floor.

  - Schlumberger Excellence in Education (SEED) Science Lab. Available at www.seed.slb.com/en/scictr/lab/index_virtual.htm.

  - The ChemCollective: Online Resources for Teaching and Learning Chemistry. Available at www.chemcollective.org.

Additional Resources

- Wikibooks: Natural Science Bookshelf. Available at http://en.wikibooks.org/wiki/Wikibooks:Science_bookshelf.

- Wikibooks: Physics Bookshelf. Available at http://en.wikibooks.org/wiki/Wikibooks:Physics_bookshelf.

FIELD RESEARCH PROJECT

Wikis and other Web tools have enabled field research and the collection of field data in ways unimagined ten years ago, from online learning adventures that follow an Amazon River exploration (www.wildernessclassroom.com) to national bird and butterfly watches (www.birdsource.org/gbbc and www.monarchwatch.org). National wiki projects, such as the Encyclopedia of Life Project (www.eol.org), give field researchers opportunities to contribute a vast amount of data to a single, well-organized project. Field research projects take advantage of participants' distributed locations, making them excellent projects for online learning.

Purpose

Small or large groups can conduct a field study with the support of a wiki. The shared wiki space allows multiple field researchers to collect data for group analysis and discussion, and supports both qualitative (observation and interviews) and quantitative (survey and measurement) data collection methods. Use this approach when your learning outcomes emphasize data collection and analysis skills. The approach also helps to generate discussion about the diversity of data collected from different settings and environments, and can be particularly enlightening in social science and psychology courses.

Frame

In many cases the wiki will be primarily used as a shared location where field data will be collected, summarized, and discussed for an already designed research project, although the group can also use the wiki to collaboratively design the research project. In this case, structure the wiki so that instructions for data collection are clear and provide sufficient organization to easily view and interpret the data.

Home Page   The project home page should provide a clear introduction to the research project and connect students to relevant background information. Include an introduction to the research problem, list specific research and learning outcomes to be gained from the project, and provide hyperlinks to helpful Web information and resources. If the classroom wiki is used to collect data that will be provided to a national project, include a summary and hyperlink to the project's Web site.

Guidelines for the Collection of Field Data   Clearly define the data collection method(s) to be used in the project, and provide printable checklists, forms, or instruments to support the collection of consistent and reliable field data. Ensure that the data collection instruments match the wiki pages in which researchers will record and share data. Provide clear instructions to student researchers regarding who, when, where, and how field research will be conducted.

Data Summary and Analysis   The structure of the wiki pages in this section will vary based on the data collection method. For qualitative methods, such as observation and interviews, you will need at least one page per student for the raw data to be documented. Create additional pages to analyze patterns and themes in the data. For quantitative methods, such as measurement and surveys, you will need to embed tables or link to a wiki spreadsheet (for example, using Google spreadsheets), in which students can complete their data entry. Spreadsheets allow you to apply simple formulas, such as sums and means, to the data for analysis.

Discussion   The discussion following data collection will lead to the deepest learning from the project. Provide a page on which students can both ask and answer questions regarding the data. Encourage students to identify themes and patterns in the data. If there is wide variation in the data collected from different field locations, encourage students to speculate on the intervening variables that may have had an impact on results.

Management Tips

- In most cases, students will need some instruction in sound research and data collection methods before embarking on a field study. Before students begin collecting data, give them information about field research methods. Then conduct an online discussion or chat session to clear up misunderstandings, answer questions, and ensure that all collected data will be usable in the study.

- If students need a jump start to begin discussing the results, provide stem statements on the discussion wiki page to get things going. For example; "One thing that this research tells us about (butterflies) is . . ."

Additional Resources

- The Research Methods Knowledge Base. Available at www.socialresearch methods.net/kb/.

STORY CREATION

Having students collaborate on a story is a great way to encourage creative writing. Wikis facilitate this process by allowing learners to brainstorm ideas, outline the process, and write their story. The story does not have to be written in prose form. Consider different types of writing, such as poetry and drama, in addition to prose narratives.

Purpose

Use story creation wikis when your desired learning outcomes emphasize creativity and collaboration. Story creation projects are excellent teaching tools for developing writing skills and reinforcing the writing process.

Frame

When structuring a creative writing project, it is important to support the phases of the writing process. This example illustrates how a group of students can use a wiki to collaboratively write a one-act play.

Home Page   This page should include a general summary of the story; a list of characters; and links to each of the scenes, with a brief description.

Brainstorming Page   Provide a page that supports the initial brainstorming and prewriting phases of the project. Encourage students to collaboratively determine the elements of the story:

- Genre, mood, and tone
- Plot and detailed outline of the scenes
- Conflict
- Character descriptions
- Setting

Scene Pages   There should be a page set up for each scene. Scenes can be developed in sequence, or smaller groups can concurrently develop individual scenes. Include a brief description of the scene at the top of the page and a link back to the home page.

Management Tips

- The whole class can work together on this type of wiki project, but it will be easier to manage if students identify their individual roles and responsibilities early in the process. For example, different students can be in charge of maintaining the continuity of the setting, individual characters, stage direction, or dialogue.

- It will be helpful to prepare learners in advance so that they understand such concepts as:
  - What is a script?
  - How is a script organized (acts, scenes, etc.)?
  - How is dialogue used in a play?
  - What types of scene directions are necessary?

- Depending on the level and skills of your students, you may need to scaffold the scene organization of the story and provide each scene with a brief description of the plot and setting. Encourage students to outline the plot or action of the scene before adding details, such as dialogue and stage directions.

- Provide a discussion or reflection activity at the end of the project to allow students to discuss insights and comments on the creative process to share their thoughts about the strengths and limitations of creative writing as a group.

- Determine in advance how your students will use the final project. Will they actually perform the play? Will you want to continue the story with future classes?

Additional Resources

- Writiki. Available at www.writiki.com/wiki/index.php?title=Main_Page.

TEAM CHALLENGE

Looking for a creative team project in the spirit of *Apprentice* or *Amazing Race*? Although it's unlikely (and not recommended) that you will "fire" any of your students after the project is complete, a wiki can be the perfect vehicle for brainstorming, testing, and developing creative solutions to real-world problems.

We are all inventors and entrepreneurs at heart. Use this wiki project when you need to rally a team and get the creative juices flowing.

Purpose

To challenge is to "arouse or stimulate especially by presenting with difficulties" (Webster's Online Dictionary, 2008). When creating a meaningful wiki challenge, choose a problem that exists in the real world and is relevant to the topic or field being studied. The parameters for a challenge can range from the realistic (develop and market the next best-selling food product) to the idealistic (outline a strategy to slow global warming). Use this approach when your desired learning outcomes include brainstorming, critical thinking, and the development of a sound strategy or solution. Although this project approach is well suited to *Apprentice*-like business challenges, it can also promote team problem-solving skills and creativity in other disciplines, such as agriculture, math, science, social science, and engineering.

The word *challenge* can also mean "an invitation to a competition" (Webster's Online Dictionary, 2008). Determine at the start of the project whether teams will compete, and if they will, how you will evaluate and reward solutions. Healthy and educational competition emphasizes fun and rewards (all participants are winners), has no lasting negative effects on students' self-esteem, and involves students in the review and evaluation process (Curriculum, Technology & Education Reform [CTER], 2008).

Frame

Framing for the wiki project must support teams in their ability to form, brainstorm, and negotiate strategic solutions.

The Challenge Present the project challenge and provide teams with links to resources that help describe the current situation and scope of the problem.

Team Charter Page The team charter page should contain the following information:

- Team name and members
- Team rules for working creatively

Brainstorming Area or Sandbox Use this area to give learners an opportunity to try out various ideas for their projects.

Team Solution The following is a possible solution framework for a food product challenge:

- Describe the product's purpose. Provide a sketch, drawing, or photograph of a product prototype.
- Describe the product's competitive advantages.
- Describe the raw materials required (optional).
- Describe the process of production (optional).

Implementation Strategies (Optional) The following example is a possible marketing strategy framework for a food product challenge:

- Product: Identify strategies that enhance the product's advantages in the marketplace. Strategies may include branding, packaging, quality control, and manufacturing process improvements.
- Price: Describe strategies for pricing. Strategies may include list price, discounts, bundling, and financing.
- Place: Describe strategies for getting the product to consumers. Strategies may include sales locations, distribution channels, and logistics.
- Promotion: Describe strategies for promoting the product to target consumers. Strategies may include advertising, public relations, and promotional programs.

Management Tips

- Encourage teams to suspend judgment during the brainstorming phase of the project. Allow sufficient time for teams to brainstorm and elaborate on ideas, without moving too quickly into the solution phase. Consider waiting to release solution pages until the forming and brainstorming stages are complete.
- Construct an evaluation rubric for the final solution and share it as part of the challenge page. The rubric should identify the main criteria on which solutions will be judged, yet still leave room for creative approaches. The rubric allows the instructor to evaluate the project and gives other teams a tool for peer feedback.
- Prepare team rewards for a variety of success factors: the most creative solution, the most practical solution, the best team collaboration, and so on. Ensure that each team is rewarded.

MEDIA DESIGN PROJECT

Media design projects are typically group efforts that focus on identifying a need and designing an appropriate solution to meet that need. These projects are meant to model real-world group processes. Media design projects work well in wikis, which allow group members to monitor the project, conduct reviews, provide feedback to members, and maintain balanced participation and version control.

Purpose

A media design project must include the necessary documentation and steps required to move the project through the stages of analysis, design, and development. The wiki can be used as the center for collaborating on key planning documents, including the needs assessment, audience analysis, scripts, and storyboards. The wiki serves as the central location for all of the relevant documents, and can also provide a means for group members to share files, comment on progress, and manage the project. When appropriate, students can share the project with other stakeholders, such as clients, managers, or instructors. Although media design projects can vary in length and scope, typically they will include documents on:

- Analysis
- Proposals and scope
- Design
- Storyboards or scripts
- Evaluation

Frame

The Problem   This page should present the background of the project and provide direction as to what the learners will need to do. The instructor should create this page, either directly in the wiki or in a learning management system with a link to the wiki.

Analysis   There may be one or more pages detailing the front-end analysis of the problem. Learners may need guidance as to what they should provide, which will depend on the nature of the online class and the type of problem they are exploring. Typically, the analysis will include:

- Needs assessment
- Audience analysis
- Environment or organizational analysis

In addition, you may require more information that is specific to your topic.

Proposal   Once learners have completed the initial analysis, they will need to write a proposal describing what they will design and create to meet the identified needs. See Figure 5.4 for a sample project proposal.

**Figure 5.4
Sample Project Proposal**

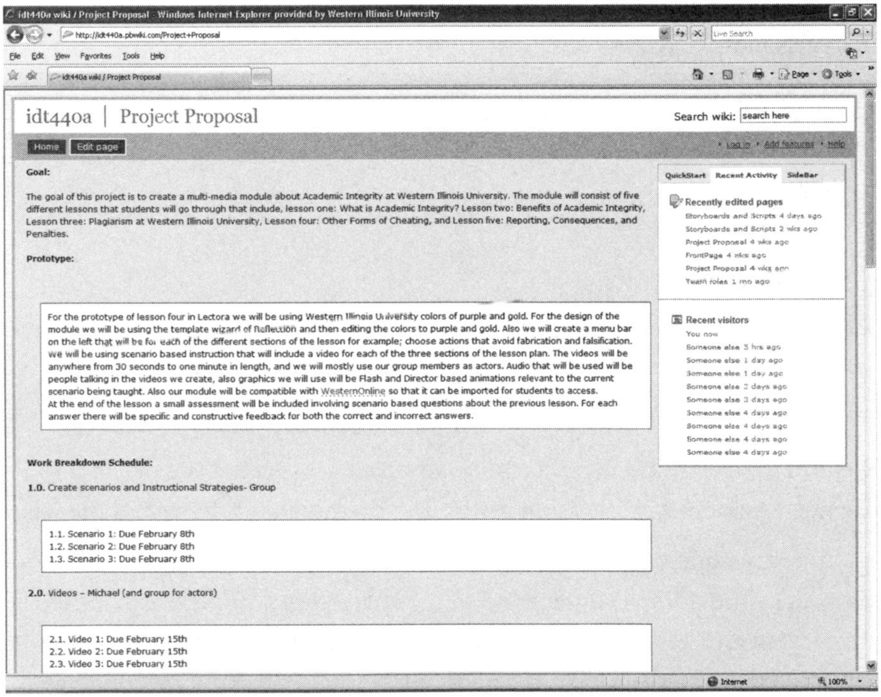

Design Documents Design documents will also vary depending on your subject matter and the nature of your class. Typical design documents may include:

- High-level design specifications
- Detailed design documents
- Storyboards
- Scripts

Evaluation Documents Once they have designed and developed the project, learners can use the wiki to report on the project's level of success. Evaluation can be either formative or summative. The following is a possible wiki frame for an instructional design project:

- Analysis (including needs assessment, learner analysis, environment analysis, task analysis, learning objectives, and assessment)
- Proposal
- Macro-level organization or course map
- Instructional strategies
- Storyboards
- Media scripts
- Formative evaluation

Management Tips

One challenge will be to ensure that groups actually collaborate on the various parts of the project, rather than using a divide-and-conquer method for completing it. You can approach this at several levels:

- Require that all group members sign off on each aspect of the project. You can use the comment or discussion features to do this for each page in the wiki.
- Include assessments, such as quizzes, on each aspect of the project to measure each individual's understanding of the group's project as a whole. The assessment can test students on specific information contained within each group's project, rather than on generic questions. Ask, for example, "What are

the specific learning outcomes that your group identified?" rather than "What are the components of a good learning objective?"

- Use the wiki's version control feature to identify each member's contribution to his or her group. This information shows not only who made contributions but what those contributions were.

- Ask group members to use the wiki's blog, journal, or discussion features to explain their specific contributions to the project.

- Clearly state your guidelines for collaboration and use of the wiki.

- This type of project may require considerable time between deliverables; therefore, group sign-offs or progress updates should be fairly regular.

SERVICE LEARNING PROJECT

Service learning is the pairing of academic study in the classroom with student service for an organization outside of the classroom (Canada & Speck, 2001). Sometimes referred to as experiential learning, action learning, or university-community partnerships, these experiences integrate theory and practice, and foster a deep understanding of community, social, and civic issues.

Wikis offer unique possibilities for service learning. A wiki can provide a shared space for students and community agencies to build information-rich public Web sites, glossaries, FAQ pages, and resource bibliographies, which promote community education and awareness. A wiki can support an encyclopedic reference resource on a social or civic issue for a professional organization or national agency. An even more ambitious wiki can support a global partnership with a sister university or global agency in order to support an international education or aid effort. Imagine a project that pairs nursing students with a local community health agency to promote women's health. Or a project that pairs a classroom of U.S. students with students in another nation to study and share perspectives on a social issue.

Purpose

Service learning builds community partnerships and extends the collaborative circle beyond the classroom. Use this approach when your primary goal is to foster responsible citizenship and promote the study of social issues.

Frame

The core pages for a service learning wiki will vary for each project and will be driven by the goals of the community partnership. However, in addition to the core service pages, every service learning project should include the following:

Introduction   Introduce the project and its overall purpose. Provide a section about each project partner and agency.

Service Learning Project Goals and Outcomes   Clearly outline the goals and outcomes of the project for both the students and the community agency. With student input, define student learning (cognitive) and personal growth (affective) outcomes. Use the page to collaboratively define, negotiate, and refine the service goals with the partner agency.

Student Roles and Contributions   Similar to event planning, the service learning project will require project planning pages that support the identification of teams, tasks, logistics, and timelines for student service and contributions.

Reflection   Proponents of service learning agree that reflection is the most critical factor in the success of a service learning project, as it is the element that ties the service to the learning (Rubin, 2001). Provide a wiki page with reflection questions, to which students can collaboratively respond throughout the project. Students can also use the commenting or discussion features available in most wikis for reflection.

Management Tips

- Determine early on if the service learning project will be a single-semester or multiple-semester project. Often a community need cannot be addressed in a single semester. If a project spans semesters, group the student roles and contributions pages by semester and identify benchmarks for each phase of the project.

- Be resourceful in identifying community partners. Seek assistance from campus development and career planning offices to identify established university-community relationships. If this search is not fruitful, contact a central community service agency, such as the United Way (http://uwint.org/devfinal/), to identify community groups that may have a need and are willing to work with students.

- Solicit support from, and partnerships with, other faculty and students in your college (or in other colleges) to accomplish larger service projects. Always look for opportunities that extend the collaboration beyond the classroom.

- For extended service projects, consider a local server installation of a wiki (such as TWiki or MediaWiki), rather than relying on a free wiki service. This choice will offer more stability and greater control over the wiki structure and its contributors.

Additional Resources

- Learn and Serve America's National Service Learning Clearinghouse. Available at www.servicelearning.org.

- Campus Compact Service Learning Website. Available at www.compact.org.

- Appropedia Wiki: Service Learning Portal. Available at www.appropedia. org/Service_learning.

- EASLwiki: The Encyclopedia of Academic Service Learning. Available at http://servicebook.org/faculty/wiki/.

SUMMARY

Contextual application projects allow students to apply and integrate skills in a real-world context. The wiki projects in this chapter require students to gather information, concepts, and theories, and to apply them to new situations or problems. Framing a contextual application project includes ensuring that students are given the right tools and support structures necessary to brainstorm, plan, and accomplish group goals. When you develop the wiki frame, you will need to consider project milestones or deliverables and make sure your wiki service provides the space, tools, and flexibility required to carry out the project successfully. In the next and final chapter, we will explore how wikis can be integrated with other tools, and explore future applications of wiki technology.

Wikis Today and Tomorrow

According to the 2008 Horizon Report (New Media Consortium & Educause), wikis are a growing presence on many college campuses. Wikis support collaboration for faculty research, staff development, online learning, and a variety of educational applications. Wiki collaboration does not require expensive equipment or Web programming skills. When framed well, wiki projects can support effective pedagogy and can promote knowledge construction, critical thinking, and real-world application of skills and concepts.

The power of the wiki is limited only by its contributors. Wikis are flexible enough to be adapted to small group projects as well as large-scale global collaborations. For face-to-face, hybrid, and online learning courses, wiki collaborations have the potential to break down the boundaries of the classroom. Wiki projects can bring field experts, community leaders, practitioners, and past students into the collaborative space. Wiki projects are scalable and can extend over time, allowing participation across weeks, months, and even multiple semesters.

THE VALUE OF COLLABORATIVE WRITING

At the heart of every wiki project is the process of collaborative writing. Collaboration is becoming key to success in a global economy. The 2008 Horizon Report states that "the way we work, collaborate, and communicate is evolving as boundaries become more fluid and globalization increases" (New Media Consortium &

Educause, 2008). Tools, such as wikis, that allow learners to work together in writing a document or creating a story help students to master collaboration and writing skills, which will transfer to a challenging and dynamic workplace.

Many learners view collaborative writing as a natural and necessary extension of their social communication skills. Today's learners "are immersed in an environment of electronic communication that is vitally important to them, but that may not necessarily lend itself to lengthy, logically structured writing" (Lenhart, Arefeh, Smith, & MacGill, 2008). Providing students with structured collaborative writing experiences can bridge the gap between social communications and the ability to write with clarity, and can have an influence on work and society. Even today, students are coming to expect collaborative experiences as a part of higher education.

INTEGRATING WIKIS WITH OTHER TECHNOLOGIES

Although new technologies for online learning are constantly being introduced, this doesn't mean wikis will be going out of style any time soon. Indeed, collaborative wiki projects will continue to grow as central tools in online courses. As the technology advances, additional features will undoubtedly be added or enhanced to make wikis easier to use and to provide opportunities for more robust activities.

Wikis are being integrated with other Web applications and tools to meet the demands of education and the workplace. "The renewed emphasis on collaborative learning is pushing the educational community to develop new forms of interaction and assessment" (New Media Consortium & Educause, 2008). Educators are already using wikis alongside other Web 2.0 technologies. Social networking tools and mashups (text, audio, video, animations, or widgets from preexisting sources combined into a new Web page) can incorporate wikis with other resources and Web tools. Communication tools, such as Web conferencing and Voice over Internet Protocol (VoIP), and mobile devices, such as the iPhone, allow for more personal connections among learners, instructors, and other experts in the field. For example, having a wiki document available while you are conducting a VoIP conference call could be a very powerful combination.

WHAT THE FUTURE HOLDS

Of all the Web 2.0 developments, the wiki is the most common collaboration tool used in online learning (Villano, 2008). Wikis are much more than an online fad. Because wikis represent the combination of three stable concepts—collaboration, writing, and constant Web access—the wiki will remain a staple of the Web and will continue to evolve in its usefulness for online education and the workplace. The following issues will have an impact on the future of wikis and will continue to expand the usefulness of the technology:

Collective Intelligence

Collective intelligence is the "knowledge and understanding that emerges from large groups of people" (New Media Consortium & Educause, 2008). Global wiki projects that attempt to tap into the creative thinking and diversity of worldwide audiences will come online in growing numbers (see, for example, www.1000000monkeys.com). No problem will be too small or too large for global input. Addressing a global problem, such as climate change, in a wiki (see, for example, http://earth.wikia.com) can provide students with opportunities not only to construct their own knowledge but also to contribute to a global solution.

Ubiquitous Collaboration

Wikis' accessibility and ease of use will extend the possibilities for online collaboration well beyond its current limits. Online collaboration will be considered in everything from product design to the planning of class reunions. Web applications that support document sharing and wiki creation "on the fly" will be integrated into social networks and communication systems. For example, many online e-mail systems are now evolving into collaborative suites, enabling the development of shared wiki pages, calendars, and contact lists, in addition to basic e-mail communications (see, for example, www.zimbra.com).

Virtual Workplace

More and more companies are relying on collaboration among physically dispersed virtual teams to solve problems and develop new ideas. Collaborative tools, such as wikis and content management systems, are enabling a transparent virtual workplace that will continue to grow in future years. Virtual teams have widely adopted wikis because they enable balanced participation from team members and are accessible at any place and any time (Mader, 2008). Students who engage in online collaboration and wiki work during their education will be well prepared for the challenges of the virtual workplace.

Multiple Language Translation

The world's largest wiki, Wikipedia, has more than thirty languages, each of which has over fifty thousand articles. Nevertheless, the language barrier still has an impact on global collaboration. Development of more streamlined and effective language translators, and wiki projects that invite users to correct and improve translations and cultural references in online documents, are on the wiki horizon.

Accessibility

The accessibility of Web content for disabled students and users will continue to be a central issue, as the Web moves deeper into Web 2.0. As asked at the International Cross-Disciplinary Conference on Web Accessibility in April 2008 (W4A, 2008), "What happens [to accessibility] when surfers become authors and designers?" Wiki tools and services will need to integrate validation tools to ensure that audiences with disabilities are not excluded from contributing to or reading wiki content.

AN INVITATION TO COLLABORATE

This book has attempted to provide practical guidelines and examples for how wikis can be incorporated into online learning. The sample wiki projects we have provided are a starting point for using wikis to enhance learning, but these are not the only examples. We have created a wiki at http://wikiframes.pbWiki.com, into which you can add your own wiki frames. We invite you to share comments and ideas in this wiki space in the spirit of collaboration on which this book is based. It is our hope that this book has demonstrated how wikis can support collaborative writing and that you find the integration of wiki projects into your own online courses to be both useful and rewarding.

The following wiki is maintained by the authors of this book. Check here for additional wiki projects or add a wiki project of your own.

- WikiFrames: http://wikiframes.pbwiki.com/

WIKIS FOR EDUCATORS

There are hundreds of wiki services available out there. This is a list of a small number of them. For information on other wiki services, check out Wikimatrix.

- Wikimatrix: www.wikimatrix.org
- Wikiversity: http://wikiversity.org/
- PbWiki Power Educators Wiki: http://educators.pbwiki.com/
- Wetpaint's Wikis in Education: www.wetpaint.com/page/education
- Google Docs Tour: www.google.com/google-d-s/intl/en/tour1.html
- Zoho FAQ: http://zoho.com/zoho_faq.html
- How Does MediaWiki Work?: www.mediawiki.org/wiki/How_does_ MediaWiki_work%3F
- TWiki Success Stories: http://twiki.org/cgi-bin/view/Main/TWiki SuccessStories

WEB 2.0

The following Web sites provide additional information on Web 2.0 technologies and how they are impacting education.

- e-learning 2.0—How Web Technologies Are Shaping Education: www. readwriteweb.com/archives/e-learning_20.php

- Educause's 2008 Horizon Report: http://connect.educause.edu/Library/ELI/2008HorizonReport/45926
- What Is Web 2.0: www.oreillynet.com/pub/a/oreilly/tim/news/2005/09/30/what-is-web-20.html
- "Web 2.0" in Wikipedia: http://en.wikipedia.org/wiki/Web_2

COLLABORATIVE WRITING

There are many online sources that provide guidelines and tips for assigning collaborative writing projects. In addition, many schools offer guides to educators concerning incorporating collaborative writing into their courses. Here are some examples.

- Teach Collaborative Revision with Google Docs: www.google.com/educators/weeklyreader.html
- Why Consider Collaborative Writing Assignments?: http://wac.colostate.edu/intro/pop2l.cfm
- Collaborative Writing Projects: www.nelliemuller.com/Collaborative_Projects.htm
- Collaborative Writing Tools and Technology: A Mini-Guide: www.kolabora.com/news/2007/03/01/collaborative_writing_tools_and_technology.htm

SCAFFOLDING

The following Web sites include discussions about using scaffolding in education.

- Scaffolding for Success: http://fno.org/dec99/scaffold.html
- Scaffolding Web Site: http://condor.admin.ccny.cuny.edu/~group4/

BLOOM'S TAXONOMY

The following Web sites contain detailed information regarding Bloom's Taxonomy, including the original and the recently revised versions.

- Beyond Bloom—A New Version of the Cognitive Taxonomy: www.uwsp.edu/education/lwilson/curric/newtaxonomy.htm
- Bloom's Taxonomy (Original and Revised): www.odu.edu/educ/roverbau/bloom/blooms_taxonomy.htm

REFERENCES

Anderson, L. W., & Krathwohl, D. R. (Eds.). (2001). *A taxonomy for learning, teaching and assessing: A revision of Bloom's taxonomy of educational objectives.* New York: Longman.

Association of American Colleges and Universities (AACU). (2007). College learning for the new global century: A report from the National Leadership Council for Liberal Education and America's Promise. Retrieved March 5, 2008, from www.aacu.org/advocacy/leap/documents/GlobalCentury_final.pdf.

Babb, P. (2007). The ten commandments of blog and wiki etiquette. *Infoworld.* Retrieved February 15, 2008, from www.infoworld.com/article/07/05/28/22FEblogwikicommandments_1.html.

Bean, J. (2001). *Engaging ideas: The professor's guide to integrating writing, critical thinking, and active learning in the classroom.* San Francisco: Jossey-Bass.

Beldarrain, Y. (2006). Distance education trends: Integrating new technologies to foster student interaction and collaboration. *Distance Education, 27*(2), 139–153.

Bloom, B. S. (Ed.). (1956). *Taxonomy of educational objectives: The classification of education goals: Handbook I, cognitive domain.* New York, Toronto: Longmans, Green.

Bold, M. (2006). Use of wikis in graduate course work. *Journal of Interactive Learning Research, 17*(1), 5–14.

Bruner, J. S. (1975). The ontogenesis of speech acts. *Journal of Child Language, 2*(1), 1–40.

Bruner, J. S. (1990). *Acts of meaning.* Cambridge, MA: Harvard University Press.

Buono, A. F. (2004). Leadership challenges in global virtual teams: Lessons from the field. *SAM Advanced Management Journal, 69*(4), 4–10.

Canada, M., & Speck, B.W. (2001). Editors' notes. In M. Canada & B. W. Speck (Eds.), *Developing and implementing service-learning programs* (pp. 1–2). New Directions for Higher Education, no. 114. San Francisco: Jossey-Bass.

Carvin, A. (2005). Tim Berners-Lee: Weaving a semantic web. Retrieved November 20, 2007, from www.digitaldivide.net/articles/view.php?ArticleID=20.

Chase, D. (2007). Transformative sharing with instant messaging, wikis, interactive maps, and Flickr. *Computers in Libraries, 27*(1), 7–8, 52–54, 56.

Conrad, R. M., & Donaldson, J. A. (2004). *Engaging the online learner.* San Francisco: Jossey-Bass.

Curriculum, Technology & Education Reform (CTER). (2008). Competition in the classroom. *WikEd.* Retrieved January 26, 2008, from http://wik.ed.uiuc.edu/index.php?title=Competition_in_the_Classroom&redirect=no.

Duarte, D., & Snyder, N. T. (2001). *Mastering virtual teams: Strategies, tools, and techniques that succeed* (2nd ed.). San Francisco: Jossey-Bass.

The educator's guide to the read/write Web. (2006, January). *Educational Leadership, 63*(4), 24–27.

Engstrom, M., & Jewett, D. (2005). Collaborative learning the wiki way. *TechTrends, 49*(6), 12–15, 68.

Facione, P., & Facione, N. (2007, March/April). Talking critical thinking. *Change, 39*(2), 38–44.

Farabaugh, R. (2007). 'The isle is full of noises': Using wiki software to establish a discourse community in a Shakespeare classroom. *Language Awareness, 16*(1), 41–56.

Fink, L. D. (2003). *Creating significant learning experiences: An integrated approach to designing college courses.* San Francisco: Jossey-Bass.

Godwin-Jones, R. (2003). Emerging technologies: Blogs and wikis: Environments for on-line collaboration. *Language Learning & Technology, 7*(2), 12–16.

Gordon, R., & Stephens, M. (2007). Putting wikis into play. *Computers in Libraries, 27*(2), 42–43.

Johnson, D. W., & Johnson, F. P. (2006). *Joining together: Group theory and group skills* (9th ed.). Boston: Pearson Education.

Johnson, E. B. (2002). *Contextual teaching and learning: What it is and why it's here to stay.* Thousand Oaks, CA: Sage.

Jonassen, D. H., Howland, J., Marra, R. M., & Crismond, D. (2007). *Meaningful learning with technology* (3rd ed.). Columbus, OH: Merrill/Prentice Hall.

Knowles, M. (1984). *The adult learner: A neglected species* (3rd ed.). Houston, TX: Gulf.

Knowlton, D. (2001). Promoting durable knowledge construction through online discussion. Retrieved March 4, 2008, from www.mtsu.edu/~itconf/proceed01/11.html.

Lamb, B. (2004). Wide open spaces: Wikis ready or not. *Educause, 39*(5), 36, 38, 40, 42, 44–46, 48.

Larkin, M. (2002). *Using scaffolded instruction to optimize learning.* Arlington, VA: ERIC Clearinghouse on Disabilities and Gifted Education. (ED 474301)

Lenhart, A., Arefeh, S., Smith, A., & MacGill, A. (2008). *Writing, technology and teens.* Pew Research Center. Retrieved July 21, 2008, from http://www.pewinternet.org/PPF/r/247/report_display.asp

Lightner, S., Bober, M., & Willi, C. (2007). Team-based activities to promote engaged learning. *College Teaching, 55*(1), 5–18.

Mader, S. (2008). *Wikipatterns.* Hoboken, NJ: Wiley.

Mindel, J. L., & Verma, S. (2006). Wikis for teaching and learning. *Communications of the Association for Information Systems, 18*(1), 1–23.

Neidorf, R. (2006). *Teach beyond your reach: An instructor's guide to developing and running successful distance learning classes, workshops, training sessions and more.* Medford, NJ: Information Today.

Nessel, D., & Graham, J. M. (2006). *Thinking strategies for student achievement: Improving learning across the curriculum, K–12.* Thousand Oaks, CA: Corwin Press.

New Media Consortium & Educause. (2008). The 2008 horizon report. Austin, TX: New Media Consortium. Retrieved April 23, 2008, from www.nmc.org/pdf/2008-Horizon-Report.pdf.

Nothiger, A. (2008). HyperHistory online. Retrieved January 26, 2008, from www.hyper-history.com/online_n2/History_n2/a.html.

Oblinger, D., & Oblinger J. (2005). Is it age or IT: First steps toward understanding the net generation. In *Educating the net generation* (pp. 2.1–2.20). Boulder, CO: Educause.

Palloff, R. M., & Pratt, K. (2005). *Collaborating online: Learning together in community.* San Francisco: Jossey-Bass.

Peha, S. (2002). The writing process. Retrieved February 23, 2008, from www.ttms.org/PDFs/04%20Writing%20Process%20v001%20(Full).pdf.

Piagct, J. (1970). *The science of education and the psychology of the child.* New York: Grossman.

Pyatt, E. (2006). Using case studies in teaching. *Penn State University, Teaching and Learning with Technology.* Retrieved February 14, 2008, from http://tlt.psu.edu/suggestions/cases/.

Richardson, W. (2006). *Blogs, wikis, podcasts and other powerful Web tools for classrooms.* Thousand Oaks, CA: Corwin Press.

Rubin, M. S. (2001). A smart start to service-learning. In M. Canada & B. W. Speck (Eds.), *Developing and implementing service-learning programs* (pp. 15–26). New Directions for Higher Education, no. 114. San Francisco: Jossey-Bass.

Sass, E. (2008). American educational history: A hypertext timeline. Retrieved January 12, 2008, from www.cloudnet.com/%7Eedrbsass/educationhistorytimeline.html.

Sharples, M. (Ed.). (1993). *Computer supported collaborative writing.* London: Springer-Verlag.

Tapscott, D., & Williams, A. (2006). *Wikinomics: How mass collaboration changes everything.* New York: Portfolio Hardcover (Penguin).

Tuckman, B. W., & Jensen, M.A.C. (1977). Stages of small group development revisited. *Group and Organizational Studies,* 2, 419–427.

University of Maryland University College. (2008). Online guide to writing and research. Retrieved February 23, 2008, from www.umuc.edu/ewc/onlineguide/welcome.shtml.

University of Michigan. (2004). Assignment assistant: Annotated bibliography. Retrieved February 25, 2008, from www.lib.umich.edu/ugl/guides/assist/assignments/annotatedbib.html.

University of Victoria Distance Education Services. (2007). Collaborative writing. Retrieved February 23, 2008, from www.distance.uvic.ca/students/collabor.htm.

Villano, M. (2008, April). Web 2.0 tools: Wikis, blogs, & more, oh my! *Campus Technology,* pp. 42–44, 46, 48, 50.

Vygotsky, L. S. (1978). *Mind in society.* Cambridge, MA: Harvard University Press.

W4A—International Cross-Disciplinary Conference on Web Accessibility (2008). One world, one Web: Surfers become designers? Retrieved July 21, 2008, from http://www.w4a.info/2008/.

Waters, J. (2007, March). Curriculum unbound! *T.H.E. Journal,* pp. 40–48.

Webster's Online Dictionary. (2008). Challenge. Retrieved January 19, 2008, from www.merriam-webster.com/dictionary/challenge.

West, J., Sample, S., & West, M. (2007). Online collaboration tools in instructional design, in *Proceedings of the 2007 Annual Conference on Distance Teaching and Learning,* Madison, WI: University of Wisconsin, pp. 250–253.

INDEX

Lightner, S., 2
LMS. *See* Learning management systems (LMS)
Lockdown manager, 52
Login, 10, 11, 14, 15

M

MacGill, A., 126
Macro map, sample, 107
Mader, S., 26–27, 52, 127
Management tips: for annotated bibliography
    project, 72; for case study project, 84; for
    class encyclopedia project, 76; for col-
    laborative research papers project, 90; for
    debate project, 86–87; for error finding
    and correcting project, 65–66; for evalua-
    tion or research study project, 93; for event
    plan project, 104; for FAQ project, 64; for
    field research project, 112; for frame-based
    writing project, 95; for group summary
    project, 74; for historical time line project,
    68; for media design project, 120–121; for
    online dialogue project, 72–73; for process
    map project, 107–108; for resource bank
    project, 61–62; for service learning project,
    122–123; for story creation project, 115;
    for structured online critiques project, 99;
    for team challenge project, 117; for virtual
    science lab project, 111; for "what if . . . ?"
    scenarios project, 81–82
Marra, R. M., 21–22
Mashups, 126
Media design project: design documents for,
    120; evaluation documents for, 120; frame,
    118–119; management tips for, 120–121;
    purpose of, 118; sample project proposal
    for, 119; as wiki project for contextual
    application, 118–120
Media sharing, 1
MediaWiki (wiki software), 7, 17, 18, 75, 123
MERLOT (Multimedia Educational Resource
    for Learning and Online Teaching), 111
Metacognitive outcomes (indirect), 34
Microsoft Excel, 12–13
Microsoft PowerPoint, 12–13, 61
Microsoft Word, 12–13, 61
Millennial students, 24–26

Mindel, J. L., 21, 35, 39
MIT Zero Waste Event Planning Guide Wiki, 104
MLA (Modern Language Association)
    Formatting and Style Guide, 70–71
Momentum, building, 47–50
Monarchwatch.org, 112
Monitoring, 53–54
Moodle (learning management system), 9, 17
MSNBC, 17
Multiple language translation, 128
Multiple user accounts, 14

N

N/3 method, 96–97
National Teaching and Learning Forum
    (NTLF), 84
Neidorf, R., 45, 46
Nessel, D., 93
Net Generation, 24. *See also* Millennial students
New Media Consortium & Educause, 125–127
Nominal group technique project: discussion
    and clarification in, 96; final rankings in,
    97; frame, 96; idea generation in, 96;
    management tips for, 98; purpose of,
    95–96; and round one of voting, 96–97;
    and round two of voting, 97; as wiki
    project for critical thinking, 95–98
Nothinger, A., 66
NTLF. *See* National Teaching and Learning
    Forum (NTLF)

O

Objective learning outcomes, 34
Oblinger, D., 24
Oblinger, J., 24
Online collaboration, 3; millennial students
    and, 24; ubiquitous, 127
Online dialogue project, 72–73; frame, 72–73;
    home page, 72–73; management tips, 73;
    team dialogue pages, 73
Online learning, opportunities for, 2
Openness, 23, 28–29. *See also* Digital
    commons; Key behaviors for learning in
OverOrganizer behavior, 52
Ownership, 23

122; and service learning project goals
and outcomes, 122; and student roles and
contributions, 122; as wiki project for
contextual learning, 121–123

Sharing, 23. *See also* Digital commons; Key
behaviors for learning in

Sharples, M., 26–27

Skins, 13

Skype, 104

Smith, A., 126

Snyder, N. T., 29

Sociability, 24–25

Social constructivists, 37, 59

Social networking, 1, 126

Speck, B. W., 121

Stephens, M., 29

Sticky wikis, dealing with, 55

Story creation project: additional resources for,
115; brainstorming page, 114; frame, 114;
home page, 114; management tips for, 115;
purpose of, 114; scene pages, 114; as wiki
project for contextual application, 114–115

Structure, 25

Structured online critiques project: and
evaluation criteria, 99; frame, 99;
management tips for, 99; purpose of, 98–99;
as wiki project for critical thinking, 98–99

Students, nontraditional, 25–26

Style guide, 70

T

Tapscott, D., 3, 23, 26–28

TeacherTube Science Channel, 111

Team assessment, 44–45

Team challenge project: brainstorming area or
sandbox for, 116; frame, 116; management
tips for, 117; and optional implementation
strategies, 117; purpose of, 116; team
charter page for, 116; and team solution,
117; as wiki project for contextual
application, 115–117

Team charter page, for team challenge
project, 116

Team process pages, 36–37

Teams, 25

Threaded discussion, 2–5

Trial runs, 47

Trust, creating atmosphere of, 46–47; and
sample trust exercises, 48

Tuckman, B. W., 45

TWiki (wiki software), 7, 75, 123

2008 Horizon Report (New Media Consortium
& Educause), 125–126

U

United Way, 122

University of Maryland, 49

University of Michigan, 69

University of Victoria Distance Education
Services, 49

University of Virginia Virtual Lab, 111

URL, 18–19, 104, 108

Users, number of, 15

V

Verma, S., 21, 35, 39

Version control, 15–16

Villano, M., 126

Virtual science lab project: additional
resources for, 111; and DNA Microarray
Virtual Lab from Wikiversity, 110; frame,
109–111; management tips for, 111;
purpose of, 109; resources for, 111; table
of contents, 109; virtual lab pages,
109–110; as wiki project for contextual
application, 109–111

Virtual workplace, 127

Vizu Polls, 17

Voice over Internet Protocol (VoIP), 56, 104, 126

VoIP. *See* Voice over Internet Protocol (VoIP)

Vygotsky, L. S., 37

W

W4A-International Cross-Disciplinary
Conference on Web Accessibility, 128

Waters, J., 3

Web 1.0, 1

Web 2.0, 1, 2, 126, 128; additional resources
on, 129–130

Web conferencing, 126

Web skills, 28